Satish Kumar is Chairman of the Schumacher Society and Editor of *Resurgence*, the journal with which Dr Schumacher was closely associated and which is concerned with fostering a long-term vision of the social change embodied in Dr Schumacher's work. His autobiograpy, *No Destination*, was published in 1978. Satish Kumar lives in Devon.

THE SCHUMACHER LECTURES
Second Volume

Edited with an Introduction by
Satish Kumar

First published in Great Britain by
Blond & Briggs 1984
Published in Abacus by
Sphere Books Ltd 1986
30–32 Gray's Inn Road, London WC1X 8JL
This Collection Copyright © 1984 The Schumacher Society

Printed and bound in Great Britain by
Collins, Glasgow

Contents

Introduction

In one lifetime we have witnessed the rise and fall of industrial civilization. The years of 'never had it so good' have come and gone. The notion that the nations can live by economics alone is under severe review. The children of science, technology and material wealth are starved of spiritual fulfilment. The same technology which provided an illusion of high living standards threatens us with the prospect of a nuclear holocaust, a prospect so terrifying that governments, industrial institutions and mainstream media prefer to remain asleep.

In the 1950s Dr E. F. Schumacher acted like an alarm clock. He started the Intermediate Technology Group, warned us of an impending oil crisis, and in the '70s he exposed the dangers of bigness in pursuit of power and profit. His well-known book, *Small is Beautiful*, woke many people from a sound sleep. Concern for our environment, for values, for Nature and for peace were the signs of this awakening. In the fields of physics, of medicine, of education, of energy, this awakening was more evident. People from within the establishment started to question the basis of our civilization. Books were written, get-togethers were organized, and people engaged themselves in a number of new projects and experiments. A strong alliance between peace with oneself, peace with the peoples of the world and peace with Nature began to be recognized. A search for wholeness and quality, together with the realization that the movement for an alternative to the industrial society may have many facets but that in essence all those facets are closely interlinked, were the hallmarks of Schumacher's thinking. He promoted peace, alternative sources of energy, organic farming, intermediate technology, tree-planting, meaningful work, a spiritual outlook and a host of other activities.

In 1977 Dr Schumacher died from heart failure. His friends and collaborators believed that the best tribute to him was to continue the work he had started. And for that purpose the Schumacher Society and the Lectures were established.

The annual event of the Schumacher Lectures in Bristol has become an important feature, not only of Bristol life but of global alternative thinking. The Lectures attract people from all over Britain. A gathering of 600 or more from different backgrounds and interests makes the Lectures perhaps the country's most prominent forum for investigating alternative ideas in depth and detail.

An informal organization of voluntary helpers, hosts and stewards has grown up which comes alive once a year to sell tickets, look after the speakers, organize the bookstall, promote *Resurgence* magazine, and a host of other activities focused on one day. The cost of the Lectures and therefore the price of tickets is kept low, as not only do the organizers give their time and attention voluntarily but so also do the speakers; only their travelling expenses are paid. They give their lectures free, and the Society welcomes them in the warmest possible manner.

An international dimension is a special feature of these Lectures. At least one, and sometimes more than one, speaker comes from abroad. In this way we are able to establish closer links with the work and thinking of kindred-spirit movements throughout the world.

But words remain empty if they are not complemented by practical action. Although the Lectures are an intellectual event, they exist only to communicate the practical implications of the ideas they express. Dr Schumacher himself would never have been satisfied were there not a strong link between words and action. Therefore the Schumacher Society is also closely associated with a number of projects of a practical nature. The establishment of the Small School in the village of Hartland is one such example. Modern education splits knowledge into fragments. It serves mainly urban industrial society and it is secular and impersonal. But it is not good enough just to criticize the present system of education and think that we have reached a solution. It is better to light a candle than curse the darkness.

The Schumacher Society is not a formal membership society. The best way to keep in touch with our work is to read *Resurgence* magazine, which is closely associated with the Schumacher Society. Schumacher himself was one of the most frequent contributors to it. Most Schumacher Lectures are published in *Resurgence*, and the activities of a large number of practising ecologists and decentralists are reported through its pages.

The Schumacher Society also runs a mail-order Book Service to promote and spread the ideas of kindred thinkers and activists. This is because it has never been the Society's intention to turn Schumacher into a cult figure and organize hero-worship around his name, any more than to suggest that his words must be taken as final. He was part of a process of holistic thinking. Many before and since have expounded a philosophy which looks at the existence of man- and womankind as a part of natural creation. The human being is neither at the centre of it nor its master. There exists a whole tradition of thinking and philosophy which puts forward ways and means of living in harmony with Nature and of limiting our material needs. This tradition of thinking in relation to our environment has moral as well as practical significance. A simple ecological and spiritual lifestyle is not only necessary for the survival of the human species, it is also more fulfilling and more satisfying.

There are other, perhaps more rational, environmentalisms, survival-orientated and basing their polemics on fear of pollution and lack of resources. But the speakers whose lectures are compiled in this collection go beyond this approach and present a more profound, immediate and urgent message.

Satish Kumar,
Schumacher Society,
Ford House,
Hartland,
BIDEFORD,
Devon,
United Kingdom.

Dr E. F. Schumacher
An Appreciation

John Davy

Fritz Schumacher first publicly launched his idea of an 'intermediate technology' for the Third World in an article in the *Observer* in 1965. He argued that advanced technology was having disastrous effects in developing countries, and a quite different approach was needed. The newspapers described his views as 'startling' and many experts were scornful.

In the spring of 1977, six months before he died, I heard him speak in Ann Arbor, Michigan, on a cold Sunday evening, at the tail end of a university vacation, to a rapt audience of 5,000 students. He had become a hero of the alternative society, a spokesman not only for some radical ideas about development in the Third World but also for the groundswell of frustration and despair, especially among the young, over the miseries of life in advanced societies.

His American tour drew huge youthful crowds. But he was also received by State governors, prominent academics and industrialists, and by President Carter. The ecological crisis and the energy crisis, of which he was an early prophet, were beginning to become the conventional wisdom of a multitude. Mr Desai's new government in India had publicly embraced intermediate technology. The American Government had set up a $20 million fund for research in alternative technologies. And in Britain official support was at last forthcoming for the Intermediate Technology Development

Group, which Schumacher founded in 1965.

The title of his best-selling book, *Small is Beautiful* has passed into the language. No man, it would seem, could ask for his life to be crowned with more success. So why did I find him, after his lecture, in a curiously uncertain mood?

In part, he was doubtful about his own success. He wondered how much real will for change lay behind the enthusiasm. He saw a danger that his words could be inflated into gas balloons, which would carry people gently over the landscape of the world's problems at a considerable height, in the illusion that their trip was changing life below. He was deeply sceptical of panaceas and blanket solutions. He saw real hope for the future in many small-scale but concrete initiatives; in his own domestic life this included milling wheat by hand and baking bread, thus bringing a therapeutic balance into the life of a busy intellectual, and providing his family with a product much superior in quality to any available in the shops.

But his real concern went deeper. He died just before publication of his latest book, *A Guide for the Perplexed*. He was convinced that the real answers to our problems would come not from new means – intermediate technology included – but from new ends. Technological society, he held, was a product of a crippled and impoverished view of human beings and of the world, which goes back in intellectual terms to Descartes, and the subsequent conviction that all important realities are measurable.

He began to ponder these questions 35 years ago, as a farm labourer in Northamptonshire. Born in Bonn, he had been a Rhodes scholar in Oxford in the 1930s and then, having decided that to live and work in Nazi Germany was impossible, emigrated to England permanently. The war brought a brief internment, then farm work until 1943.

After the war he worked with Beveridge; he was also a prominent member of editorial team at the *Observer*. From 1945–50 he was economic adviser in the British Control Commission in Germany. There followed 20 years as economic adviser to the National Coal Board in London, when he began to perceive vividly that our industrial way of life is built on a profligate expenditure of natural capital, namely, coal and oil.

During this period he was seconded to advise the Government of Burma, and managed to include some serious study of Buddhism. This influenced the now classic essay, *Buddhist Economics*.

In 1962 Schumacher spent time with the planning commission in Delhi to advise on rural development. There he saw the appalling effects of pouring in aid in the form of advanced technology. Often plant broke down and could not be maintained. But where it worked, cheap goods undercut rural industries. Unemployment in the villages brought migration to the shanty towns spreading round the big cities. The Western technologies could be operated only by an élite. The rich got rich, the poor, poorer.

From these experiences came the concept of 'intermediate technology', of the kind that in Europe allowed the long, slow transition from the Middle Ages to the twentieth century. The traditional village tools were too primitive, Western tools too complex. There was a gap in the middle – a need for simple pumps, improved building materials and storage techniques, packing machinery and tools that could be understood and maintained by a village blacksmith.

Such technologies were almost forgotten. One of the first tasks of the Intermediate Technology Group was to compile a catalogue of suitable products – *Tools for*

Progress.

The group now has a team of full-time employees, a series of expert panels, and consultancy and development units with contacts and projects all over the world, many of them highly successful. But the problems are formidable. The educated élite in developing countries, usually trained in Europe or America, tends to have been brainwashed into the same uncritical enthusiasm for technical sophistication which produces so much idiocy in the West.

Schumacher was the first to acknowledge that without human and social development, technology – intermediate or otherwise – can achieve nothing. Thus it remains to be seen how far and how deep the intermediate technology idea can reach into the problems of the Third World.

Meanwhile Schumacher's work attracted growing attention in the advanced countries. We too have unemployment generated by labour-saving technologies, decaying cities and depersonalized work. Schumacher was convinced that we are witnessing the end of a way of life that will destroy itself by its own contradictions within half a century.

In his last years, among his many activities Schumacher also presided over a society to promote organic farming and gardening, the Soil Association. This body, once widely regarded as the resort of cranks, now rates as a respectable pioneer of ecological sense. Schumacher had seen the havoc which agribusiness can create in developing countries. Now its gross inefficiencies, in global terms, are becoming clear in advanced countries.

One of his latest enthusiasms was for food-bearing trees, which can achieve three-dimensional protein production with solar energy. He launched a project to breed improved varieties, build seed stocks and promote planting, in the interests of our children, to help them survive the food crisis which he expected to be the inevitable companion of the coming energy crisis.

Towards the end of his life he was confirmed into the Roman Catholic Church (making legal, as he put it, a long-standing illicit love affair). For his *Guide for the Perplexed* he had been reading Thomas Aquinas, and often quoted his saying, 'The slenderest knowledge that may be obtained of the highest things is more desirable than the most certain knowledge of lesser things.'

On his American tour, his youthful audiences frequently tried to draw him into a denunciation of the giant corporations. He refused to be drawn. 'I never deal with corporations,' he said, 'I deal only with people. And I have actually found some very able people even inside big corporations.' He met everyone as though they really mattered. And he lived his own life with consistent humanity. He will be missed – and remembered.

This article was first published in the *Observer* and is reprinted with their kind permission.

I
Sinking with Style

Johan Galtung

Dear friends, I shall be talking about our so-called crisis, so why not start where so many people start: with oil and OPEC in 1973. The producers had for a long time suspected that the demand for oil was inelastic over a wide range of prices – so why not move to the upper end of that range instead of being below the bottom end of it?

They practised market economics: they put up the prices and discovered the demand was still there. I know from some of them that they were somewhat surprised, as a matter of fact, that so much demand *was* still there. So they did it once again. Then they were told by liberal economists that this is absolutely horrible. How can you do such a thing to us? And they said, 'But look! Samuelson's textbook on economics says that that is what you should do.' And they were told again, 'Yes, but you see, it doesn't apply in your case; oil belongs to mankind, whereas the kinds of thing that we have – technology – they belong to us. And that's a difference that you haven't understood.' Now, they still haven't understood it and they just go on, just continue.

In that type of world what is happening is very simply the following. Our time is up – *c'est fini, mon ami* – and more so the more deeply one's economy was based on trade, and particularly with the Third World, which again is a function of the extent to which one's econ-

1

omic success was based on having an empire, and also a function of the extent to which it was based on processing raw materials into processed goods, pocketing the value added. Britain fits those formulas fairly neatly – so, of course, you go down. I don't think this is a cycle, a business cycle; it is neither a short-run cycle nor a Kondratiev cycle. It is simply the decline, and possible fall, not of the West but of Western imperialism. What distinguishes Britain from many other countries is an ability until recently to take it in style, to go down in style, with grace. I myself have suggested on many occasions a 'United Nations Management Agency for Decline', the 'UNMAD'. It should be headed by an executive director (who could be a Briton . . . not Madame Thatcher, I think . . . possibly Lord Soames, who is a man for many purposes, but I think Lord Carrington would actually be the best one) and could put Britons at the disposal of other countries in decline on a *per diem* basis. Some sense of humour is needed, because not all countries are able to change the national anthem from 'Rule Britannia. Britannia Rules the Waves' to 'All You Need is Love' in only about 20 years. Britons have a sense of humour still. What crisis?

I suggest that the world economic situation is not in any sense turning against capitalism, so far. There is no crisis at all in the world capitalist system – but there is a crisis in the Western control-position. These two statements have been held by many as contradictory because it has been assumed that to manage anything as world-encompassing and as complicated as world capitalism is a Western prerogative. Now, in that underlying faith – shared by liberals and Marxist thinkers alike – there is a solid amount of white supremacy and racism. As they system is changing now, under the new international economic order, those control-positions are being undermined. That does not mean that there is not going to be a new centre. Personally, I think that the new centre is already emerging, and it is emerging exactly at the opposite end of the world. Like the old international economic order was run by a triangle constituted roughly by the United States, the European Community countries (with appendages, like my own – Norway) and Japan, I think there is a new triangle emerging which is constituted roughly by China, Japan and South-East Asia – perhaps with Australia and New Zealand in it. As a matter of fact, it is interesting to see that a very clever little country – Japan – has been able to be in both triangles, even at the same time; it takes some talent to do that.

Why didn't Britain do that? Maybe because they were not talented enough. Maybe they were too complacent. I am saying this because the world is changing. Basically, I don't think we are heading into a future where it is possible at the same time to increase labour productivity through automation and robotization, substituting ever more research- and capital-intensive technologies for the ones we have, and to give more and more employment to more and more people – and at the same time be able to survive economically. I think that is only possible on the assumption of an expanding market. With 149 other countries trying to do the same, there might be some difficulties for some of the countries in the classical West in attempting to continue to do so. The rest is a question of power: who is going to be able to get what market share? That power is not only in military and political terms; it is also certainly in economic, technical terms. One simple reason why people are now riding Japanese motorbikes and not British ones around the world, or buying Japanese watches and not Swiss ones, or using Japanese cameras and not German ones, could be that Japanese goods

3

are both better and cheaper! If this is levelled against the Japanese, they might also say that they have read Samuelson and a couple of other books and found in Samuelson that, if the consumer has a free choice, such things as price and quality would matter to him.

In short, other parts of the world are now playing what used to be our game, and playing it better. The Japanese even have the audacity now to produce Sanyo music machines (just to take one example which I saw in Mongolia some months ago) as good as ever but made in the People's Republic of China. There are 600 million workers in China. Very diligent. They are infused with the same Confucian, Buddhist and Oriental (if I may say so) work attitude as the Japanese. It may be that this will also give a slight competitive edge to that part of the world.

I think we have been through all of this before in Western history. The similarities with the decline of the Roman Empire are very important, but in this there is not necessarily a dark message of pessimism. With the decline of the Roman Empire came things that were not good for the parasitical leaders of Rome. During a period of some centuries the population of Rome shrank from almost 2 million down to 20,000. Those 2 million were to a large extent parasites who, like most people in this room including myself, never produced anything material. In order to make that equation work they had to do something which is very similar to what we have been doing.

They had to exploit in four directions at the same time. Number one: exploit an external proletariat (in Toynbeean terms), namely the provinces of the Roman Empire. When Spain managed to liberate herself from the Roman Empire, her standard of living went up. Number two: exploit the internal proletariat, the slaves. When the Roman Empire went down some

4

centuries later, the successors to the slaves – the serfs – had on average a higher standard of living than the slaves had done. Number three: the rapacious exploitation of Nature. This was done in ways that have been commented on and documented very well. The deserts, the bad fields of the Maghreb countries of Northern Africa, are still, 2,000 years later, to a large extent the sad outcome of anti-ecological practices, of the way the corn was ground in order to be shipped to Rome, to be the *panem* part of the *panem et circenses* formula. And there it was eaten, and it went down the sewers into the Mediterranean, and that was where the fertilizer went instead of being recycled back to the ground from which it was taken. And then there is the number four, which the Roman Empire didn't have, and that was a very high level of productivity.

The first three worked relatively well for some time, but they did not have the fourth one that is based on technology. They were not, one can say, motivated in that direction. But we have been stuck with the current OECD formula, which has been the current OECD formula for the last couple of years. With the internal proletariat there isn't much we can do, for they are too strong. They have trade unions, labour parties, and they are quite clever at organizing strikes. We are not living in the 1830s. With the external proletariat there is also not so much we can do. The Third World is getting strong now. The new international economic order has shown its muscle through OPEC and others. And when it comes to Nature we are also in a difficult situation. It is quite clear that there are limits to growth, as the slogan ran in the beginning of the 1970s. In addition to that, there are all these Green movements. When Nature doesn't tell, you have all these Green, ecological people, running around telling it for Nature.

So what about high productivity, which we need to become once again competitive on the market? The difficulty with high productivity is, to my mind, the following. Of course we can increase productivity. Of course we are capable of doing it. Of course we are capable of transforming science into technology and ultimately to a large extent eliminating labour through automation/robotization. But there are five problems that come up, and those five problems are rather essential: the five basic costs of high productivity.

One: if for labour we substitute capital, research and administration, then we get a society that is capitalist, researcher- and administrator-intensive. Please note that I change here from the economist's way of talking to the sociologist's way of talking. I don't say 'research-intensive' – I say instead 'researcher-intensive'. Instead of 'administrator' let us call him or her a 'bureaucrat'. So we get a society which is bureaucrat-, capitalist-, researcher/intelligentsia-intensive – 'BCI'. That society we know; it is a society of technocrats. That's fine for those people – and since many of them are in this room, I could almost say it is fine for *us*. The only problem about it is: what does it leave for the rest of the population? It gives to the BCI-complex the possibility of relatively unalienated work, because the BCI-complex will have the privilege of processing uncertainty into decisions, as administrators, as the managers of capital, or as the researcher, who is the manager of problems – of processing problems and finding a formula for their solution. That is great – it is exhilarating, it gives meaning to life to many.

But the more people there are who do this, the more people there will be on the other side whose task it is to carry out their instructions, and their work will either be non-work, with compulsory free time, or it will be meaningless work. And here comes then the basic point

– and that has to do with the meaning of work. This is exactly what Schumacher explores in his admirable chapter, 'Buddhist Economics' (which perhaps is neither quite Buddhism nor quite economics, but it doesn't matter – it should be both and it is a brilliant chapter): the basic point in working being that it offers a possibility of realising your own faculties and a possibility of getting into a context with other people and being socially useful in that context. Take these two away from people and you reduce the *homo faber* at most to a *homo ludens*, a playful little thing whose task it is to sit in front of the television, or to sit in a football stadium, or to watch football on television. Since the World Cup is only every four years, one very reasonable prediction is that with increasing labour productivity we shall get an increasing frequency of World Cups in order to be able to substitute them for work – say, a World Cup once a week. Why not? In other words, a higher Cup productivity – so that one can substitute entertainment intensity for work intensity.

Now the transformation of *homo faber* to *homo ludens* presupposes that on top there is the BCI-complex, which is then the *homo sapiens* component that arrogates and monopolizes to itself the right and privilege to have unalienated work administrating and clientalizing the rest of the population: a vicious Utopia of Keynes! My first two items on the list of costs of productivity are the following: point one, the top-heavy BCI-dominated society; point two, unemployment disguised as compulsory leisure for the rest of the population. We have come quite far in that direction already, and I would like to mention one particular person who is responsible for much of this. He happens to be a Briton: Lord Keynes – a great intellectual, admirable for many things. But if you read his essay written in 1930, *Economic Possibilities for Our Grand-*

children, he has what I think is essentially an extremely vicious Utopia. It is a Utopia 100 years hence. It is written during the Depression, and he says, 'All you people, don't be so depressed. There are good periods ahead of us. Good times will come. I have happy news for you. In 100 years hence we'll get a society where work is down to three-hour shifts or a fifteen-hour week [to kill something he called "the old Adam in most of us"]. It is not strictly necessary to have even those 15 hours, but this old Adam [there is nothing about old Eve] . . . this old Adam wants to do some work all the time – so, OK, give him 15 hours to keep him busy. The rest of the time we shall use to compose poems, make paintings, engage in arts, read poems for each other, etc.' I think he also thought that there would be those who would write books in that period – like he probably would. So what is wrong with that?

Well, what is wrong with it seems to me to be one extremely basic thing. It could be, first of all, that not everybody likes to write poems or listen to poems. It could be, for instance, that this is a professor's sabbatical year projected on the rest of the population as the compulsory Utopia for everybody. It happens that I like it, but I don't think that I have a right to say to everybody that this is what they should do. It may be that other people express themselves in other ways. Secondly, there is a terrible class connotation of a society catering to the faculties and the interests of some particular type of people, unless you do assume that all interests and abilities are absolutely evenly distributed, which seems to be a rather unrealistic assumption. I honestly do not think that we know today in any sense what is the ideal load of work that everyone wants to have, and I think it is a telling indictment of our social scientists that we don't know about it. But I think it is quite clear that just as much as we deplore and hate the conditions that were applied to children and women and men for instance, in this country (and you do not have to go back to Marx's description), we very much celebrate the fact that there are labour-saving devices that make it possible to escape from heavy, dirty, degrading work. But this is only one end of the scale. There is another end of the scale where there is the enforced absence of work. This very idea of keeping people in the school ghetto long beyond any time they want to be there, then giving them a short lapse of work, and then pushing them out and into the old-age ghetto: all of this is some type of structural fascism.

There are extremes of this. One extreme is what is known now as the Danish solution (where unemployment among youth is very high), which is to keep people at universities till they are 45 and then pension them off immediately. It has great advantages. They do not constitute any pressure on the labour market at all, and in the first 45 years they can go the People's High School and discuss such problems as the crisis of unemployment, and the next 45 years they can continue in that People's High School – only they are called 'pensioners' by that time – and have courses in exactly the same problems. But all of this is a caricature of a society. Let me only say that at the end of the Roman Empire there were a couple of things that happened that are interesting. First of all, the sons and daughters of the élite, and some of the élite persons themselves, did what élites do: they made use of the privilege of being an élite person to protect themselves. The mechanism of protection was quite interesting. They simply left Rome for the countryside, and in the countryside they built something known as the *villa Romana* – I would say a sort of big self-sufficient complex, a kind of big farm. It was constituted by those élite persons

9

together with their serfs, and what came out of it was to become the medieval manor later on. The former slave was persuaded to join this on the condition of receiving the type òf freedom he got as a serf, which essentially was that he had to stay in the same place all his life, and so had his sons and daughters – but he could not be sold and he could not be bought. In other words, he was no longer a commodity. One sees immediately some similiarities to today. If you want to know when a system is coming to its end, then one good indicator is when the élite is moving to the countryside. In other words, all you have to do to watch it is to stand at Paddington Station and look a little bit at what happens and do it, let us say, at one-month or one-year intervals. And by that I don't mean weekend trips; there is a continuous process here – there are persons who start with two days in the countryside and five days in London and then, through a period of 10, 20 or 30 years, it becomes five days in the countryside and two days in the town. There will be houses in the capital converted into studio-houses, where you have one little room in the city for that day.

In this connection, a new, frightening class perspective comes up, similar to the Roman situation: the gap between those protecting themselves through escape versus those who cannot escape. To see this more clearly, let me now mention the last three arguments against increasing productivity.

They are the following: the three 'civilisation diseases'. They are called 'civilization diseases' because they come with a particular social construction of which a core concept is exactly 'high productivity'. They are: point one – mental disorder; point two – cardio-vascular diseases; and point three – malignant tumours, or, in other words, cancers. The aetiology of these three is certainly not sufficiently known, but by and large we know that the search for a virus that one can seek and destroy has been no more successful than the perennial American search for communist agents that can be sought and destroyed. It comes, incidentally, out of the same expansionist and slightly Christian-tinged paradigm: the idea that at the margin of the system there are evil forces at work, and those evil forces should be destroyed.

It seems, however, that the evil forces are at the centre of the system and that the best we know today is that the aetiology is linked to two particularly important factors. One is what we often call 'stress', that arises from a social structure that is very, very vertical, very heavy and demanding, and the other one is 'pollution', that arises from the new environment for human beings, made up of non-natural compounds in different compositions and ratios, that our bodies simply seem unable to take. It is also a telling indictment of our natural scientists that they have not been able to predict this in advance. That 'the carcinogenic agent of the week' seems to be the same surprise every week tells us what extremely bad natural scientists and medical researchers we have had.

There are reasons for this. The vested interests in increasing productivity are tremendous, and for that reason the system needs people who have the following characteristics: they should be able to see the necessity of high productivity, but also be blind to the following: point one, international politics; point two, history; point three, culture; point four, Nature: point five, human beings. If you are blind to all these five but very perspective on productivity, then you have a key to a career. What kind of people are these? Well, my favourite scapegoats are, of course, economists – and if you find that statement racist, then it *is* racist. It is *absolutely* racist! I would even suggest a sort of bleeper on all economists so that one knows where they are at all times. Fritz Schumacher was something of the best you can find in that profession today – a former economist.

So, I am suggesting that we are on a course away from a system of yesterday to which we cannot return, and which politicians for that reason divide, roughly speaking, into two categories: those who think it is possible to return, and for that reason are trying to do everything they can to recreate the conditions they think obtained in the golden sixties or whatever, and those who understand that there is something irreversible in the process and that we have to look for something new. I think it is terribly important to see very clearly that the choice is of that nature.

I mentioned that up till recently Britain has been taking this in grace and style. What has happened in the last years is unfortunately something much more threatening. And that is the perspective that with the decline of the Western control-position in the system of capitalism/imperialism and the corresponding decline of the Soviet construction – the Kremlocentric pyramid – both super-power systems at the same time may at one stage come to the conclusion that war is a lesser evil, that a war is preferable to seeing one's own system disintegrate totally. I do not think any of the super powers would like to see destruction come to their own countries. What do they do in that situation? They do what seems to me to be within their scheme of rationality, the only rational thing to do: they see to it that as high a proportion as possible of the belligerent activity in a possible nuclear war takes place outside their own territory – that means on European soil. How do you get the war to take place on European soil? By having on European soil sufficiently attractive targets – and how do get that? By persuading so-called allies to take on the maximum they can of the nuclear load. The key function of the projected cruise-missiles in Britain is not to be fired. It could be that its major function is to be hit. If collective suicide is what one is aiming for, then go ahead, acquire them. For that reason I support entirely – 150 per cent, or however many per cent you want – nuclear unilateralism in this country and in any other country. And I would like to just add one thing. It is NATO policy, and it is American policy, to use nuclear arms first in case of a non-nuclear attack with which they have difficulties. The US has so far threatened using nuclear arms on at least eight occasions since Hiroshima/Nagasaki (in Khesanh, for instance, in Vietnam) and they got away with it. As long as that is US and NATO policy, we live an extremely dangerous life, and it is all a part of the excessive imperialistic greed of the two Western systems. If we are able one way or the other to get away from this Sword of Damocles over us, what are the likely further developments in our part of the world?

Perhaps the answer is an appreciation of Buddhist cosmology. And I shall try to frame that answer by simply asking a question: why are we the way we are? We – *homo occidentalis*? I do not think there is a genetic answer to that. I think it is quite clear that any human being can be socialized into any culture – which is like any human person being able to talk any human language, not all of them but some of them. There is something in Occidental culture – the word 'paradigm' has been used; I use the word 'cosmology', and I would like to mention six points that seem to me typical of Occidental cosmology. I would like then to mention the antitheses of these six points, which seem to me typical of Buddhist cosmology. But this is not a propaganda speech for Buddhism – it is only so as to make a couple of points that seem to me to be important.

The six points that seem essential are the following, starting with the concept of space.

The Occident can be roughly described as the area dominated by the religions of the *Kitab*, the Old Testament: Judaism, Christianity and Islam. The Occident has a space concept, with itself in the centre and the rest of the world as a waiting periphery. In few places is this as clearly expressed as in *Matthew 28:18.20*, where Christ says unto the disciples, 'Go ye all out and make all peoples my disciples.' Not a very modest message . . . The radiation of causality from the centre in the West to the rest of the world – the *ex occidente lux* – has been a complex shared by liberals and Marxists alike. The terrible Marxist mistake in their thinking, of arrogating to themselves the idea that Western European history is the prototype of universal history, is a typical example. Engels even says that; even within Western Europe there are nuances. He has doubts about the Slavs, of course, that we know. Also about the Latins, because they are lazy; and about the Nordic people, because they are dirty, berserk and drink too much – which is absolutely true. However, he says there is some hope for Denmark because, as he says, to talk another language of Fritz Schumacher, 'Die eigentliche Haupstadt Danemarks ist nicht Copenhagen sonderm Hamburg' ('The real capital of Denmark is not Copenhagen but Hamburg.'). This slightly Teutonic arrogance we on the margin of the Teutonic area can recognize when we hear it, and we are slightly sensitive to it. Very Western – as Western as a transnational corporation with its headquarters in the West and its whole system radiating out to the periphery. In the periphery, in transnational corporation daughter-companies in the free-trade zones in South-East Asia, you find them busily at work, offering the workers better conditions than neighbouring national companies do. But they are doing something else in addition, which is equally interesting; they are transforming the concept of a worker from a quarrelsome, disgruntled British male, 55 years old, weighing 75 kilos, muscled, sour-looking . . . to an 18-year-old Malay girl weighing, roughly speaking, 32 kilos, not very muscular, and they are offering her a cosmetic course, treating her well after working hours to make her pliable. When she is 22 and has this habit which women have, namely of getting pregnant, then: out! In this kind of system the space concept of the West is very much at the root of our imperialist habits; it makes our imperialism look natural and normal.

And so is number two, the time concept – the idea of progress, the idea of growth. The essence of it is the 'better' idea, often expressed as, 'More is better' – a very simplistic, mathematical function: if X is good, 2X must be at least twice as good. This gives us a rectilinear graph; and the more optimistic idea that it *could* be even better than you would get for the rectinlinear curve, which gives us an exponential one. More linked to wisdom is the idea so fundamental in the whole Buddhist time concept, that whatever you have is good up to a certain point, and then it starts getting not so good. We get negative returns, a bell-shaped relation. The closest the West can come to that, or the closest, let us say, an average Western economist can come to that (to continue my racist pursuit), would be the logistic curve where growth approaches a saturation point which it cannot break through, nor is there any decline. This is important because if you think of the world in those Western terms, you will just go on and on and on with no sense of the optimum point. The antidote to this then, *la voie moyenne*, the middle road between two extremes, is a very useful guiding light, as we in the West are so extremely bad at identifying the optimum and always aim for the maximum.

Schumacher's intellectual, fantastic contribution was precisely to bring the whole concept of size to the forefront as a variable, arguing forcefully against the maximum. The Chinese are also very sensitive to size, or at least they were. In the *Directive* founding the people's communes in August 1958 – a remarkable document – was the idea that the people's commune should have a maximum of 10 to 15 thousand families. Why not more? Because they wanted some type of direct interaction. The Chinese are now in a more Occidental period, stressing the Occidental aspects of their complex civilization. I am pretty convinced that they will go back to the other aspects again in their zigzag course through the 20th century. And when that comes, incidentally, the Mao paintings may be taken up again; please note that those paintings were not burned – they are stored. Practical people, the Chinese. I shall enter a bet which I might lose: I am pretty sure they won't kill all the Gang of Four, because they will need a couple of them later in this decade.

Number three: the conceptualization of knowledge. Both in Aristotle and particularly in Descartes, there is the idea of atomization of complex problems into manageable units, attacking one or two variables at a time, and one thus arrives at the basic atom of Western understanding: the 'X–Y relation'. The curve function can be complicated, but typical of it is the detachment, the isolation of a part of a totality from the whole. Then comes the second aspect of Western epistemology, a very peculiar way of putting the detached parts together again, in something called theory-construction – an intellectual exercise in pyramid-building based on deductive relationships. One very good thing about the Saxon intellectual culture is that British intellectuals, from a Continental point of view, seem to get fatigued the moment the pyramid comes five centimetres above the ground, because it becomes 'speculative', whereas the Teutonic, the Germans, get a corresponding fatigue the moment the pyramid is rooted in reality, because there is something 'messy' about data.

Now these things belong to the varieties of Western culture because they are both based on fragmented knowledge which is, of course, the exact opposite of the Buddhist wheel. The idea of Buddhist epistemology seems to be the circular relationship, which I would like to illustrate with one little example. It is said about Einstein that he once took the train from Berne to Zurich, and of course he didn't ask, 'Does this train stop at Zurich?' He asked, 'Does Zurich stop at this train?' One would expect this from a man of his calibre. But that is not yet Buddhist epistemology. Buddhist epistemology would take the two statements, 'This train stops at Zurich' and, 'Zurich stops at this train', keep them simultaneously in their mind and let them mutually enrich each other till they constitute a non-contradictory unit. This whole thing, which is so important in Buddhism, of holistic, dialectical understanding, seems to be of basic importance.

Number four: relations between human beings and Nature. It is difficult to tell how the West got the idea that Nature can be destroyed. The Bible has both aspects to it, but it probably has something to do with the way in which Christianity distributed soul and made human beings (not all of them) entirely 'besouled' and the rest of the world, including animals, entirely 'desouled', with non-whites and women at times one, at times the other. In the non-Occidental faiths there is less of that human/nature asymmetry. Once that was done in the Occident (and that was not with Christianity – it came long before that), it became very easy to eat animals, and one of the leading Chinese theories why we in the Occident are so aggressive is precisely that we eat too much meat. This, incidentally, also from a Chinese point of view, explains why we smell badly, according to the Chinese. If one manages to kill and conquer and eat animals, to take the rest of Nature might not be that difficult.

The notion of supremacy, of course obtains also in the next point, number five: relations between man and man, woman and man, woman and woman. It attains a highly fascist form in, for instance, Hitlerism. I guess the way we treat animals, if we see history from animals' point of view, is the same way that Hitler treated so-called inferior peoples. From a Buddhist point of view, as Schumacher has said, one has to make use of some of Nature's gifts, but there are certain conditions of respect for Nature, and some of those conditions point in the direction of vegetarianism. This is not necessarily a Buddhist stance – it could also lead in the direction of very balanced types of eating.

It is obvious that if this kind of ecocide continues, then that in itself would ruin the basis for our existence. It is also obvious that if the basic relationship of extreme verticality in the way society is organized continues, then what happens is that that verticality will only be reproduced in a new form. There is not much difficulty in having left-wing governments constitute a society where instead of a private-capitalistic élite, a state-capitalistic élite comes in its place, and the old clientelism becomes instituted in new forms. The tragedy of what happened to Marxism in Eastern Europe is exactly this. What happens today in Poland, and what is the essence of the Polish workers' revolt, is a socialist revolt in a state-capitalist society, an effort to challenge the new verticality. The essence of the *21 Demands* is precisely this – point one, workers' control over what is produced, over conditions of production and how the surplus is made use of, from the factory floor up to the planning commission – and, point two, first priority to fundamental needs of those most in need. Those two points are at least *my* definition of socialism, and when it is pointed out, as it is pointed out by many, that there is a compatibility between Buddhism and socialism, it is exactly because in Buddhism the idea of controlling collectively your own work-condition is almost a religious sacrament, because work is the way in which you enrich yourself together with other people. At the same time it is a way in which you realize your own faculties. Buddhism was not only a reaction against the sheer wealth of the Hindu society, but also a reaction against its extreme poverty and, in some cases, its self-inflicted poverty. The middle way was between those two, entirely compatible with the thinking of so many people to the left and in the Green movement – of the minimum level of basic needs, and the maximum level of basic needs: the floor and the ceiling.

Number six: the concept of the transpersonal. In the Occident it is characterized by faith in a personal god, a god who is for the whole world and universal but, on the other hand, exclusive – he is the only one, and he is a he. Everybody is endowed with a personal soul, and for that soul there is the possibility of an eternal life. Imagine that you believe in those five things. What would be more natural than a universalistic conception of the world, a world steered from a centre, of a frenetic, hectic, individualism in order to acquire salvation in one's own life? There is an inner consistency between the articles of faith for Western Occidental religions and the centre/periphery construction of the world – the idea of growth, the way we organize our knowledge, the way we organize our relation to Nature, as if we were given by God the right to be the god for Nature – and the way we organize relations to other peoples, to the other sex, to other age-groups. I think by and large that the Roman Empire was the way it was because of this. There was an inner programme that should be implemented – what the French call a *project* – and I think British imperialism was the way it was for the same reason. There was a programme, a code, which was not doubted as the unchallenged assumption of the construction. I would say it was not capitalism. I would say that capitalism was the 16th- to 18th-century implementation of that programme. The British imperialistic form, like the French, was another expression, which was combined with capitalism. The poor Germans did not quite make that one, but for that reason, right now, they are a little bit better off than you British people; they were fortunate enough not to have colonies that they could lose. It took the same form, of course, for the Eastern branch of the Occident, the social imperialism of the misguided Soviet empire.

The kind of situation we are in now in the West is a crisis and, as the Chinese say when they use their famous two characters for crisis, it means, 'Danger plus Opportunity'. The danger is obvious. The opportunity seems to me to be that of using the crisis to create a better society. In that better society I think the political movement of today has made most contribution in the Green wave. By the Green wave I mean, roughly speaking, the following components. Number one: instead of exploiting the working class, much more co-operative enterprises with a social structure of factories, abolishing the distinction between labour-buyers and labour-sellers, through the establishment of co-operatives. Number two: coexistence with the Third World, and giving up this concept of competing in exporting things to the Third World. There are still a couple of things that can yield revenue to a Western country, such as study places at the LSE, and I understand they are now 'exported' at higher prices. Number three: the whole ecological movement, the whole respect for Nature. Number four: a lower, not higher, level of productivity, not by returning to the Middle Ages or the Stone Age, but a lower level of productivity in the sense of more respect for artisan-like, labour-intensive, creativity-intensive production in some fields. We need a good discussion as to which are the sectors where we still may want high productivity and which are the sectors where we can decrease it.

In short: more manual work for all of us, be that a kitchen garden or whatever. Some consciousness of an upper limit to material comfort – for instance, at the place where material comfort gives you more trouble than joy: a rather basic Buddhist insight. Perhaps a less predictable pattern for the future. Perhaps more possibility of organizing life with a less tidy life-cycle. Why should we have childhood first, then education, then work and then retirement? Why could we not start with three years' childhood and then one year's work, some education, then some retirement, and then go on as we feel like, with all kinds of things? Why should we have a dependency on capitalist production patterns when the Green economy and the informal economy could be doing so much for us – meaning, by 'informal economy', production for own consumption, production for exchange through barter, and production for exchange against money, but in very small, limited economic cycles. However, when this happens in my country, the bureaucrats come in and want to tax it, and you are supposed to put it on your income-tax return, otherwise they are not green but have a black economy. The capitalists do not like it because it means you won't go

21

to the supermarket, and the bureaucrats do not like your not going to the supermarkets because they want to tax the supermarket for the profits. Quite clearly there is a conflict here, but what are the rules of the game of that conflict – how is it fought?

I stop at that point. This locates the crisis of the West as a conflict, increasingly acute, between status quo forces that believe the past can be recreated, as given in centrifugal, expansionist Western cosmology, and forces that not only oppose those in power, but oppose the very code.

All I am suggesting, then, is that in this search much inspiration might be found in a Buddhist cosmology according to which:

Space – is more symmetric, with no centre, no periphery;

Time – is less discontinuous, less dramatic, more from eternity to eternity, not all focused on one brief episode in time;

Knowledge – is more holistic, more dialectic;

Person-nature – relations are more integrated, more respectful, less anthropocentric;

Person-person – relations are more horizontal, less individualistic;

Person-transpersonal – relations are more human, less 'in God we trust', more focused on our own striving together towards higher levels of enlightenment.

I thank you for your attention.

II

Work and Employment*

Shirley Williams

Unlike many of you I never knew Fritz Schumacher and I never had a chance to listen to his speeches, although I have heard a good deal about him, especially from the people associated with the Intermediate Technology Group.

I suppose my path to thinking that there was a good deal in what he had to say was a very different one from theirs. Many years ago now I taught in West Africa and I remember being surprised to see that the equipment which was sent as part of the aid programmes of the Western world and of the Soviet bloc consisted of huge, sophisticated machines for making roads, for laying down macadam, or for removing large quantities of topsoil – indeed, one batch even included snow ploughs. That batch was from the Soviet Union where no doubt they thought it was a good idea to have snow ploughs in a package of roadmaking equipment – but it didn't make a lot of sense in Nigeria, or the Ivory Coast, or Ghana. For the first time I thought that perhaps this wasn't very helpful, especially since all these great machines, after being a lot of fun to play with, mostly came to a dead stop after about a month, full of sand and other bits of the local environment, with nobody really able to mend them. I was struck by

---

* This lecture was delivered in 1981. Statistics refer to that date and not to the date of publication.

23

the fact that a hundred wheelbarrows or a hundred small diesel-engined tractors would have been a more valuable contribution. Perhaps even a well-bred bullock would have been a better idea in some of the fields of India than the tractors that bogged down in the mud. So that was where I started thinking about the ideas that Schumacher espoused.

Some years after that I went to Iran. I escaped with some friends, one of whom could speak Farsi, from a rather boring discussion about inflation and left in a bus early one morning before the authorities got up, to look at a number of villages in the area around Shiraz, in southern Iran. All these villages had one blessing they had never had before – a source of clean water. This is easy to dismiss if you have had clean water all your life – but if you haven't, it's very important. This was something that Shah had brought them: it meant they were able to drink water without having to boil it, or distill it, or take chances with their children's health.

This was about their only blessing, however. After that, what one learned was that the small and stony fields of Iran had been taken away from the peasants and turned into huge agri-businesses, mostly run by powerful Western companies on a very large scale indeed. The peasants with their small, stony fields – which had in the past at least fed a couple of goats and the odd sheep – looked enviously at the large farms, which benefited only the young and strong among them, for whom they provided work. The middle-aged and the old were simply expendable. That's not sentimentality – it's simply true.

So, little by little, the White Revolution of the Shah actually undercut the whole structure of the society upon which it depended. It was of course a conservative revolution – a 'White' revolution, not a red or a black one. It claimed to be a revolution growing out of the traditions of Iran, yet the revolution destroyed the very traditions from which it grew. So to me it is not altogether surprising that the reaction in Iran has been one of turning back to the roots of that society, to Islam, to small-scale farm ownership, to the Persian tradition.

There are many lessons in this. It is easy for the industrialized West and the industrialized Soviet bloc to destroy fragile cultures completely, then to wring their hands when they reap the inevitable results of the destruction of such cultures. We have done it for a long time: to the Maoris of New Zealand; to the Aborigines of Australia; to the tribal cultures of Africa; and in many other parts of the world. But one of the things we have to learn is that in interacting with the rest of the world we must interact in a way that has respect for cultures which – to adapt Schumacher's words – have embedded in them all kinds of traditional wisdom.

It would be easy to say that, and then say no more. But to do so would not tell the whole story. One of the things I have learned about politics is that politics above all is about choice, mostly very difficult choice. Politics becomes a dishonest business when politicians try to pretend that choices don't have to be made; that there aren't any priorities to be chosen; that somehow it can all be resolved by making enough promises, and by raising one's voice loud enough.

But one must face the fact that there are difficult choices. I have talked about the destructive impact that advanced, sophisticated technology has had on some of the cultures of the world – and not only on the world's cultures, but also on the world's resources. As you all know, the Sahara grows by about one kilometre in circumference every year and, as this happens, hundreds of square miles of cultivable land are destroyed. We are cutting down the world's forests so fast that it's an open question what the climate of this world will be like by the end of this century. We are so dependent on wood and fossil fuels that the temperature of the world's surface is increasing; it is at least probable that, with an average rise in temperature of about two or three degrees, the Sahara would grow not at its present rate every year but very much faster.

There is another side to the question, however, and this is what makes it so difficult. There is no doubt that Western technology has brought many blessings to the world. Let me take one example, also from my own experience. When I first went to Accra, in Ghana, I saw open sewers there, three or four feet deep, carrying human and animal sewage. Furthermore, during the rains these flooded. Not too surprisingly at that time only three children in four reached the age of five. One of the blessings that Western technology has brought to other parts of the world is unquestionably the blessing of that simplest of all technologies – plumbing. It has also brought the blessing of public health, and there are others too: without doubt, knowing how to keep foodstuffs reasonably clean and fresh for weeks at a time is a blessing; knowing how to dry grass is a blessing; knowing how to prevent insects and birds getting at and ruining crops is a blessing; and knowing how to protect whole populations against diseases such as diphtheria is a blessing.

What I am trying to say was expressed more eloquently, though not in quite the same terms, by Maurice Ash – that essentially technology is *neutral*. It is neither good nor bad in itself. It is the use that is made of it that is crucial. And, essentially, what technology does – even technology concerned with nuclear power – is to raise the quality of choice, of inescapable political, social and moral choice, to higher and higher levels. As technology progresses, with every decade

26

and generation the power available to the human race grows, and as this happens so the stakes involved in choice increase – but this power does not help us make the choices.

I want to relate all this more precisely to our own economy and to the problem that is with us all the time – unemployment. I accept completely that the basic assumptions – or as Maurice Ash calls them, 'the paradigms' – of the world economic structure have changed dramatically in the last ten years. There is no need to recount the details of this change, but let me just remind you of some aspects of it: the price of oil has increased in real terms by a factor of six since 1973; the price of energy-related raw materials, food and metals has increased in parallel with this; and the position with regard to growth in the Western world and the Soviet bloc alike – and Maurice Ash is right to note that the word 'ideology' is hardly appropriate in this respect, because both share the same industrialized and technological ideology, even though they do not share the same political ideology – has changed as both groups of countries have suddenly seen themselves confronted by the end of growth. The projections of the Organization for Economic Co-operation and Development (OECD), which all through the 1960s and early 1970s projected a rate of growth of about three to four per cent a year, in 1980 projected rates of growth of one per cent or nothing . . . or even, with regard to Britain and the United States, negative rates of growth, the first negative rates of growth we have seen, give or take the odd hiccup, since the end of the second World War.

So, it's a different scene. Politicians who have lived for a very long time with the assumption that growth would eventually 'like a rising tide float all ships' – to use the words of the late President Kennedy – now find themselves unable to see a tide that will float any ships at all.

At this point, however, I part company with Maurice Ash. I part company with him because I think that the last 30 years have not, by any means, constituted a disaster. I have to say that for very many people in the world, though especially for many people in the Western world, the quality of life has simply been better in the last 30 years than it ever was before. Far more people enjoy music; far more enjoy secondary education; far more read books; far more get holidays; far more enjoy good health; far more children live to maturity; and far more people travel. I believe all of these are unassailably good things. It is therefore by no means clear that the last 30 years has been simply a descent into a terrible form of life. It hasn't. It would be so much easier if it had, because then the whole of society would say 'Save us from that!' – but they don't.

The great majority of our fellow citizens would like to see greater material wealth. They would like to see a further improvement in the standard of living. They would like to see more economic growth. So, what do we do? First of all we have to tell them, 'Yes, you're right about this, but it's not very likely.' We have to explain that the prospects don't look like that, and that we are going to have to make choices about improving the quality of living and the quality of our environment that do not involve the mobilization of huge amounts of extra resources.

As a democratic socialist, I believe that we ought to continue to plough a great part of our Gross National Product into social and public expenditure. But it would be both foolish and dishonest for me not to recognize that the demands on public expenditure in our present structure are almost illimitable, and that therefore we have to look at the problems by looking at the structures and not just at the external balances.

Emerging from this problem of no more growth is the problem of massively increasing unemployment. Because growth and employment have been linked together, we have managed to avoid massive unemployment, until six years ago, in the industrialized world, both West and Soviet alike, by dint of demand managing to keep pace with growing productivity. But demand has been falling together with growth, and consequently we face the prospect of mass unemployment – not temporary mass unemployment, but sustained mass unemployment. By the end of 1980 there were 26 million unemployed people in the OECD countries, Europe, North America and Japan. This is the most by far that we have had since the Great Depression of the 1930s. The figure represents about 8½ per cent of the OECD's total labour force.

Such unemployment is not, nor ever will be, homogeneous, because certain groups suffer very much more than others when unemployment rises.

First of all, the young suffer. Unemployment is about two to three times higher among people under 25 than among those over 25. Why? Because society has been so organized by both business and the trade unions that the possession of a job today is the possession of a quasi-monopoly, protected to some extent by the law. It's much more difficult to get a job than to lose a job. This may sound odd when we are living in a country where jobs are being lost in thousands day after day. But beneath those lost jobs are thousands of jobs that are not being created, and for all those who lose jobs there are many more who cannot get jobs . . . almost twice as many. Unemployment among young people in the Western world was about 14 to 16 per cent in 1981 – nearly twice what it was in general.

Secondly, among unemployed young people, on the whole women suffer more than men, girls more than boys. In most countries girls are slightly less favoured for jobs – but, oddly enough, not so much in Britain where we don't have equal pay. But in those countries where equal pay has nearly been achieved, unemployment among girls is more serious than among boys, among young women than among young men.

Thirdly, among those young people and among those young women, the sufferers above all are ethnic minorities and the educationally disadvantaged: those who only have seven or eight years schooling, or in Britain a bare ten years but with nothing beyond compulsory schooling, with no form of training, no form of transition from school to work – these groups suffer the most. So we are looking at ratios of one, for general unemployment, to two for youth unemployment, to perhaps four for unemployment among ethnic minorities, and among the educationally disadvantaged. This is not a world in which to be unskilled. Nor is it much of a world in which to be semi-skilled. For the skilled it's just possible to hope to get a job in the future.

What is to be done? I for one am totally unsatisfied with the idea that we simply head on in this direction and say to ourselves there is nothing we can do, except – dare I say it – offer that favourite remedy of the reasonably comfortable middle classes: Education for Leisure. Education for Leisure is absolutely fine if you have got an education which enables you to enjoy all sorts of elements in leisure, like travel, like books, like music, like the theatre, like being part of voluntary groups and so on. But education for leisure is just a bad joke if you are talking to people in the urban ghettoes of Liverpool, New York or Manchester, because leisure (for them) means twiddling their thumbs while the years go by. Go into any of our great windy council estates and see the way in which unemployed young people spend their time. They spend it aimlessly, because nobody has given them anything much to do. They sleep late; go out to meet their friends so they can hang around together; and they watch television. Unemployment benefit affords few other diversions. Their lives are even more empty than those of people with the dreary jobs that this society quite rightly regards as dehumanizing.

So what can we do? There are several things we might do. We in the industrialized Western world and the Soviet bloc are now ill-adapted to knowing how to deal with human beings, above all with large numbers of human beings. We have been compelled by the argument that it is economically advantageous to replace a man or a woman with a machine, or an element of energy, or raw material, or land. Labour is penalized in a way that no other factor of production is penalized. For example, almost all the costs of the welfare state – social pensions, social insurance, unemployment benefit, and in most other Western countries, though not so much in Britain, the costs of health – are loaded on the back of labour. The resulting 'National Insurance Contribution' has become a fact of life, and we make the cost of employing an individual from 40% to 80% higher by financing our social security in this way. This is a major factor militating against full employment.

There are many rigidities within our societies that have caused us to move towards great concentrations both in industry and in the labour market. This is particularly true in Britain, where we have among the most concentrated industry of any country in the industrial world. It is not as true of other countries which have done a great deal to encourage small-scale businesses and small-scale enterprise in both the private and the public sectors. In Britain this pattern of concentration, allowing great trusts and mergers to build up, has created a triarchy of imperial structures which bargain with one another – big business, big unions and big government – and only adapts to change with great difficulty.

High unemployment among young people is not a passing phenomenon. I want to turn now to some of the things that we might be able to do, and to consider the relevance of Fritz Schumacher's ideas. The most popular solutions include ideas like shortening the working week, shortening the working life, extending holidays, or having paid education leave. None of these ideas is to be scorned – they all make an important contribution – but alone they are not enough. If you reduce the working week by five or ten per cent, it makes almost no difference at all to employment. Early retirement can be introduced, on a voluntary basis, but if that does not yield enough extra jobs it has to be done compulsorily, which creates heartache for those who are active and healthy and are forced not to work because they have reached the age of 55 or 60. Also, people will find ways round such restrictions – by joining the unofficial economy, getting another job, or going out and doing some work in the social services. They won't remain unemployed if they don't wish to remain unemployed. A most striking example of this occurred in the United States, when a well-meaning attempt by a group of senators to reduce the retirement age from 65 to 60 produced a colossal backlash in the form of a lobby, referred to as 'Grey Power', which swept away all the compulsory retirement provisions entirely and replaced 65 with 70 as the retirement age.

Reducing working life is not the complete answer. What we have to do as well is to look – in the tradition I think of as Schumacher's legacy – at the whole question of the mix of the factors of production: labour;

energy; raw materials; land; capital. In the last ten years all but two of these factors of production have become much more expensive. The two exceptions are labour, and information or knowledge, on which of course the micro-electronic revolution is based. Energy has already become much more expensive. Land is rapidly becoming more expensive. And raw materials are beginning to become more expensive – and as Third World countries continue to stagger under the burden of huge debts we may see them having to fight back by gradually forming powerful bargaining groups to force up the price of the goods they produce – the copper, the cocoa and the other raw materials that the West and the Soviet bloc have treated for so long as cheap goods we could expect to go on being cheap.

Where does this leave us? We have to look again at the mix of factors and at the bias against employing people instead of machines. Let me give you a few examples of what I mean. We tend always in the economic world to measure our achievement in terms of efficiency and productivity, primarily in terms of only one factor: labour. This means that a man who works on a farm in the United States where there is only one man for perhaps 400 acres will be regarded, by the measure of labour productivity, as much more productive than the man in Japan or China who works on 20 acres. But if you view it the other way round, and you look at the productivity of the acre of land instead, then the acre in Japan is much more productive than the acre in the farm in the United States.

What I am trying to say – and it requires only a small leap of the imagination – is that we ought to break away from always treating the productivity of labour as the measure, and instead treat the productivity of all the factors of production together as the measure. This means that, as land gets scarcer, we begin to move towards the criterion of the productivity of land as the crucial one and not the productivity of the men and women who work on the land.

The implications are easy to see. Regarding productivity of land as the criterion means that you begin to move towards the garden concept of agriculture rather than the industrialized concept of agriculture. It means that you begin to look at how to build up the quality and richness of the soil instead of trying to discover how you can mine the soil for what is valuable in it, leaving the soil weakened and impoverished behind you. It means moving towards fish-farming rather than fish-hunting (as mankind in many parts of the world has moved towards animal farming and away from animal hunting).

In the case of agriculture, what this means – and this is why in the end Schumacher's ideas are going to win – is that we will move gradually towards something that looks more like the self-sustaining agriculture that Schumacher talked about, rather than the exploitative, mining, industrialized agriculture that characterizes at the moment so much of the world. It is not only the politicians, however, it is also the public to whom the politicians are accountable that have to be persuaded and educated, because the two go together in a democracy, and the one cannot go very far beyond or lag very far behind the other . . . which makes the problem all the more difficult.

A second example relates to energy. I have already said that the energy : people : capital ratio has changed, to the detriment of energy, which has simply become too expensive. But there are two ways of making the energy equation balance.

You can do it by building power plants, fast-breeder reactors and the like, and by doing so you will produce the extra output of energy that you need to balance the account between demand and supply. It's a rather dangerous way to balance the account, given that we still don't really know how to dispose of radioactive wastes safely, and given another fact that is perhaps even more important: that we don't really know how to maintain, over decades, the extraordinary quality of precision engineering that is needed to make a nuclear power station absolutely safe. It isn't the risk of plutonium exploding that's the problem – it's the possibility of engineering failure in nuclear power plants that poses a very great question about how safe they are. Three Mile Island was about a human failure, a human factor. The issue is human failure, but we are human beings: we never get it completely right; and so we have to be very cautious about a technology that we haven't perfected, which relies too much on avoiding human failures. Certainly we shouldn't make ourselves more dependent on it than we need to be.

The alternative is that we have to look again at energy conservation. The government could have balanced the energy supply/demand equation here in Britain not by advancing a major power-plant programme of fast-breeder reactors and nuclear power stations, but by embarking on a major scheme for insulating existing housing and building stock – and in doing so thousands of jobs would have been created for unskilled and semi-skilled people. These would not, incidentally, be awful jobs, because every house, every building is different, each requiring a different approach, each requiring slightly different decisions to be made. They would not be just the boring, mind-blasting business of working on an assembly line – they would give a lot of people hope and they would do so on a basis that again meets the true economic needs. So, the energy/labour equation can also be made to balance, like the land/labour equation, by looking at it a different way round.

A third example I want to give you is the example of capital intensiveness versus the use of people. The whole of our thinking in our society and in government (regardless of party) has been colossally influenced by our failure to think about the extent to which we encourage the one at the expense of the other. Let me give some straightforward examples. We give tremendous allowances against profit or revenue for capital investment. A firm that invests in capital can write off the cost of most of that capital against corporation tax in this country, for example, or against profits tax in other countries. Sometimes it can produce the capital for 40 or 30 per cent of its true cost. There must, after all, be some encouragement for investment. But the fact is that in almost no countries of the West, with the single exception of the Federal Republic of Germany, do we similarly encourage the development of human capital. If an employer goes out and replaces all his employees with ten machines, his assets will be shown to increase. If his employees are trained to be more skilled, to be more capable, to be more able to take part in decision-making, to be better employees his account will show no increase in assets. Improve machine assets and a grateful country will allow employers to show an increase in assets. Improve human assets and an ungrateful country will not allow employers any benefit at all. This is part of the equation between human beings and machines, and it shows a big bias towards machines.

As we move towards large-scale technology it becomes more and more difficult to deal with human beings. Very big companies are often characterized by poor communications and bad industrial relations. Smaller companies rarely have anything like the same problems. The strike record of Britain or Italy or the United States shows that the great majority of time lost is in a certain limited number of companies, almost all of them at the 'very large' end of the scale. This is commonly because communications are so bad, so impersonal, that they simply break down. This is a particular problem in Britain where there are few effective formal structures of industrial democracy or consultation.

A fourth example is that we are beginning to find, increasingly, that small firms are better job creators. The great success story in this area is actually the United States: between 1975 and 1979 the United States created 12 million additional jobs – that is *net* additional jobs. If the same proportion had been created in Britain over the same period we would have had 3 million additional jobs today, instead of which we have lost (net) over 100,000, and more are being lost all the time. The United States created four-fifths of those 12 million net additional jobs in service industries, and more than two-thirds in establishments with less than 50 people in them. The striking thing is that the United States has a much larger small- and medium-sized business sector than we have in Britain and than there is in many other countries of Western Europe, let alone the Soviet bloc.

In some countries there are some exciting experiments going ahead in the field of creating small-scale and community enterprises both in the private and in the public sector.

In Britain, local enterprise trusts have begun to spring up in many parts of the country. The St Helens Trust, to take one example is backed by Pilkingtons and other local companies, the St Helens local authority and the West Merseyside County Council. In the last few years this has produced over 650 new jobs at a cost of about £600 per job in direct costs and about £2,500 in indirect costs, including capital lent which will have to be paid back. These jobs cover a wide range: some are in industries like printing; some are in businesses like producing shrimps for export; some are in precision manufacturing, for instance making contact lenses, also for export; and some are in businesses such as producing vegetables for canteen use and so forth – all kinds of activities, and these are permanent jobs. I must stress that these jobs cost directly about £600 and indirectly about £2,500. In contrast, the cost to a government in the West of producing one new job is in the order of £20,000 (1980 figures).

In France recently the French government passed a law which enables men and women who are unemployed to draw in advance six months' unemployment benefit together with their redundancy pay in order to use it to actually purchase back the very company that made them unemployed. This may sound odd, but 7,000 new enterprises started in France in the first year the law was in operation alone, financed out of these advance unemployment benefits – 7,000 new enterprises, thousands of permanent jobs.

In Denmark, in the public sector, community enterprises are being started. In the islands and the more remote villages of Denmark these community enterprises started life rather like our own Youth Opportunities Scheme, essentially as ways of creating work for young people without jobs. They have been so successful, mostly making craft goods – furniture, small-scale engineering equipment, repairing, recycling and so on – that the Danish government found themselves embarrassed by the fact that the local communities came in and said, 'We want to buy their products.' This was not possible, because the enterprises were in the public sector and their products were meant not to compete with the private sector. The Danish government has now decided to allow these public enterprises – these small-scale public enterprises – to flourish, to create jobs in the craft and small-scale manufacturing sector, and there again thousands of new jobs are being created.

I come last of all to the example of the Highlands and Islands Development Board, which is one of the most successful public enterprises – again, it is relatively small-scale, human, dealing with small communities, having a kind of independence in terms of development that is normally refused to bureaucracy and to civil servants. The Highlands and Islands Development Board is part of the public sector, as was the National Enterprise Board, and both escaped many of the rigidities that are so often associated with government. They have let people go out and learn from local communities, and the result of this has been the setting up of nine or ten industrial co-operatives in remote parts of the Highlands, all of them flourishing successfully and many of them bringing life back to communities which were at the end of their tether.

I believe very strongly that we can in fact create far more good, useful, valuable, significant, human jobs than we realize, and that we do not need to bow the knee to a permanent regime of unemployment . . . what has been described as an equilibrium of underemployment. I also believe that politicians are infinitely more willing to listen now than formerly. They have been frightened, but they are more willing now to listen than they have been for a very long time.

A re-examination of our assumptions about the use of labour in contrast to energy, to land, and to capital, will have repercussions for higher education – for a higher education system in which time and again men and women are trained to the use of tools, to the use of techniques, to the use of processes, but are barely trained to manage, deal with and live with other human beings. It means changes in our departments of design and architecture, so that people stop designing buildings for the pleasure of winning competitions in architectural magazines and instead design buildings that people want to live in. It's a harsh fact that most people don't want to live in housing estates and blocks of high-rise flats. They much prefer to live in rehabilitated, modernized, terraced houses, tenements, and so forth – because that is a human scale of living, and that is what they want. At last this is beginning to happen. It also means changing our management courses so that we teach people how to manage in an open and participatory way alongside other human beings, rather than desperately trying to get rid of the human beings and put something else in their place.

In the fourth Rita Hinden Memorial Lecture, which he gave in 1976, Fritz Schumacher said, 'Once a process of technological development has been set in motion, it proceeds largely by its own momentum irrespective of the intentions of its originators. *It demands an appropriate system*, for inappropriate systems spell inefficiency and failure.' Unquestionably the process of substituting the other factors of production for labour has its own momentum, and has created a system of presumptions which very few people have yet questioned, though they are beginning to do so. There is, however, no inevitability about it. Human beings should control economic systems, but for a very long time, historically, economic systems have shaped and controlled human beings. The industrial economies are still subject to a mystical readiness to accept the social consequences of economic 'improvement' (so-called), even if that economic improvement entails unemployment and impoverished lives for millions of people. The argument for doing so is much weakened when an adequate economic standard has been established. And this goes back to the other side of the equation I mentioned earlier. The argument for doing so – that is to say, making human beings subordinate to technology – is in my view destroyed completely if it can be shown that advance need not entail unemployment at all. We are slaves of our own traditional assumptions, of old ways of looking at the world, and it is by changing the old ways of looking at the world that we can convert not only politicians but also the public they are accountable to and ought to serve. If we achieve that, we shall be coming close, as Fritz Schumacher was, to the situation once described by the comment, 'Nothing is so powerful as an idea that has found its time.'

III

Energy Futures: Appropriate Scales

Gerald Leach

In the month of Fritz Schumacher's untimely death, which I have the great honour to commemorate here, I talked one night with another provocative thinker, Vladimir Kollontai, reputedly Lenin's son. Our subject was how to bring desperately needed energy to the poor in the two million villages of the Third World. While I recited the now familiar litany of the virtues of renewable energies running off the sun, the wind, animal wastes and plants – everlasting sustainability, environmental benevolence, small-scale diversity and flexibility, cultural compatibility – Kollontai asked a disturbing question. What about justice? Divide your energy sources into a million decentralized fragments, and the locally powerful may take them over. Distribute energy from a central source, symbolized, in the rhetoric of the alternative 'soft'-energy and decentralist movements, by the giant power station run by a technocratic élite, and society can, in principle, by many means, guarantee equity and fairness.

I tell this story not to glorify centralized bigness but to warn that in energy, as in most things, the real world is rarely as simple as one would like it to be. Renewable energies, appropriately modest in scale, obviously have a part – in the energy futures of developed and developing countries. But such a statement is rather different from the sweeping either/or generalizations that are now polarizing the great energy debate.

42

An influential movement now asserts that the only fundamental priority of energy policy is to develop renewable sources as rapidly as possible; and the smaller and more decentralized, the better. These small 'soft' technologies are claimed to have many virtues but, above all, to be socially appropriate because they are ideally matched to the 'alternative society' of decentralized, diverse and self-reliant life-styles. Together with energy conservation, they are also supposed to have sufficient potential to sweep away all big, centralized energy systems controlled by 'them' instead of 'us'; not only the forbidding 'super hard' technologies of nuclear power that are the only very long-run alternatives to living off the sun but also, in the meantime, the giant extraction and distribution systems of oil, gas and coal.

If you think I exaggerate, consider the reaction of an anti-nuclear campaigner to the news that a demonstrably safe, leak-proof, economic and proliferation-proof nuclear system had been developed – only it was too large to fit into anything but a national grid. From my experience of mental surgery on nuclear critics, they would still object to nuclear power on the grounds that it was too large and centralized. Many solar enthusiasts also dislike big solar stations putting power into the grid.

I intend here to question some of these cherished mythologies of the soft-energy and soft-society movements. Hold them against the harsh realities of the world and its energy problems, and many of them – however full of hope they may seem – crumble away.

Big may be beautiful. To the Third World villager relying on a windmill which he cannot repair when it fails, electricity from the city may appear more sustainable and renewable than the wind. Small may be an illusion. How can the villager get that windmill or its spare parts except through the vast networks of national and internatonal skills, production and trade? So much for the isolated self-reliance of the rural commune dream. Even renewability itself is in question. Many of the plant and forest resources now widely advocated as the greatest of all everlasting energy fixes for rich and poor countries may be all too easily depletable and simply not there when needed.

To begin this exploration of realities, I shall start with the industrialized world and some good news. One victory for the appropriate scale on which to view energy has been the 'revolution of disaggregation'. Ten years ago energy consumption was almost universally regarded as a huge and seamless lump: so many millions of tons of coal-equivalent to be supplied by expanding this fuel supply or that. Today, thanks largely to OPEC, the viewpoint has been reversed. People and their diverse basic needs for energy now hold the centre of the stage. Adopt that viewpoint and one soon sees the many ways in which those needs might cease to grow because of saturation of desires – let alone voluntary frugality – and the myriads of possible ways of meeting needs more efficiently with no sacrifice in well-being. As a result, and also because of expected energy scarcities, higher prices and lower economic growth, projections of future energy needs have almost everywhere been falling steadily and dramatically. Figure 1, taken from a June 1980 review by the US Department of Energy, is a remarkable confirmation of this point; especially as some of the lowest projections are by some prestigious establishment names.

However, we have to remember that none of these low-energy futures are certainties. They are possibilities which all require enormous and sustained changes in political will, institutional structures, technological

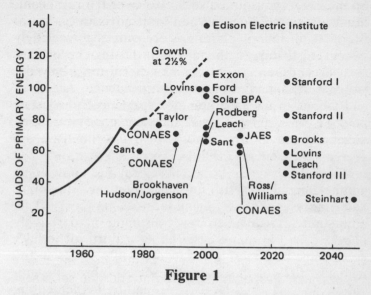

Figure 1

directions and the perceptions of millions of individual actors in the energy game.

They also involve important but conflicting issues of scale: at what level, from central government to the village or street, will change begin and should decisions be made? In some cases it is clear that local actions may be the key. An outstanding example is the production of combined heat and power: CHP, or cogeneration. Instead of turning 100 units of fuel into about 30 of electricity and throwing the rest away as waste heat, as in a conventional power station, one can recover something like 80 per cent of the original energy by piping the heat to homes, offices and factories. The economics are complicated, but often very favourable. Yet even where they are clearly attractive, large centralized electric utilities are normally reluctant to act. What they know about is building power stations; why should they get into the messy business of digging up the streets, rerouting traffic and connecting pipes to hundreds of buildings? When local government takes the lead in energy planning, or owns the electricity system, CHP surges ahead – as in Denmark, Sweden and parts of Germany. In many other ways, from providing buses and bikeways to offering advice, incentives and labour to insulate homes, experience from many places is showing that local actions can create the innovations and the framework for extraordinary progress in saving energy.

But will the really large energy savings come from another direction? With most energy-using equipment and processes, known techniques can now or will be able soon to reduce energy consumption to roughly one half, and in many cases about a third, of today's level. Most of these big reductions will come from the technical fixes of the industrial society: through innovations by small and large firms, and by implementing present knowledge through cost-reducing mass production by the large and giant corporations. It will be they who produce in the millions required the 60-or-more-miles-per-gallon cars, the heat pumps, the electricity-frugal cookers and freezers, the low-energy houses and the solar collectors of our future, more energy-thrifty, societies.

The business world is already beginning to move in these directions from self-interest. And if they move too slowly, I suggest it will be the even larger and central institutions of national government groupings, such as the Common Market (as well as popular pressures), that drives them faster. Mandatory standards and future targets for energy efficiency, taxes to raise energy prices, larger financial incentives for saving oil and other fuels, and many other regulations are now increasingly urgent items on their agenda, and are likely to be the truly powerful agents of change towards low-energy futures.

If the low-energy future appears increasing likely, what of the thoroughly soft and renewable energy futures that could lie beside or beyond them? Will they really be as soft as enthusiasts suppose?

Many exploratory sketches for these soft-energy futures are now appearing. None are predictions of what will occur; more importantly, they are tentative tests of possible futures based on a daring question. Is it feasible, in principle, to overturn completely the dependence on depleting fossil fuels that has underwritten global development for three centuries and to avoid their replacement by nuclear power, without returning to the deprivations of the past?

· Their motivations are mixed but are essentially based on three social criteria. First, there is the obvious one of sustainability to meet the needs of expanding populations. Second, there is the reduction of environmental damage, or the risk of it. Third, there is compatibility with a usually loosely defined set of social goals and development paths. The third criterion is usually given greatest emphasis but is the hardest to pin down. What it usually amounts to is the set of social goals desired by the author of the soft-energy study, which he or she rarely articulates. Nevertheless, from most soft-energy sketches some common threads repeatedly stand out. One is the promotion of local and national self-reliance versus outside dependency; don't trade but, wherever you can, do it yourself. A second is the transfer to people of control over energy supplies. Here the explicit assumptions are that large, centralized energy systems are likely to mean élitist control by remote bureaucracies, and that renewable energies, in contrast, are not. A third widely expressed assumption is that large, centralized systems are inherently more vulnerable to failure from technical breakdowns, strikes, terrorists, or other sudden disruptions. Renewable energies in contrast are assumed to share the robustness and stability of natural ecosystems that comes from a diverse and varied multitude of individual units. Fourth, there is a striking convergence around the idea that, for poor countries in particular, a mix of renewable energy sources is the most compatible with development strategies that start by meeting basic needs first, and continue by emphasizing equitable distribution rather than merely maximizing economic growth. In short, soft-energy futures are essentially about the cardinal issues of appropriateness and scale.

But are these assumptions realistic? Let us look at some of these future maps, beginning with the indus-

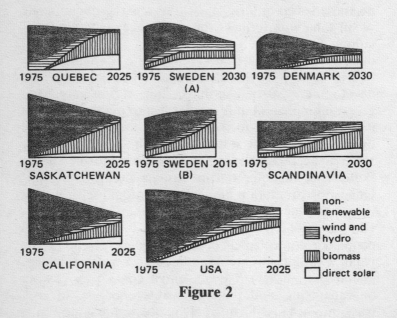

Figure 2

trialized countries. Figure 2 shows a fairly typical selection of soft-energy paths for a variety of developed regions, large and small.

The first, obvious message is that in most cases energy consumption falls substantially. That could happen, as we have seen, with varying social implications. However, the cynic's immediate response is that as energy demand begins to fall substantially, all the conventional economic and political pressures to sustain that fall and also switch massively from fossil to renewable energies will ease off. What degree of popular pressure or government determination will be necessary to maintain the momentum towards soft-energy futures? And what, in pluralist, democratic societies are the implications of that?

The answers are not known yet. However, the pioneering work by the Swedish Secretariat for Future Studies on the political implications of an all-nuclear or all-solar future for Sweden suggest that they are not simple. Their main conclusions are that it is technically possible to meet an energy demand slightly above today's by either option. Although there are large uncertainties on either side, the financial costs appear to be much the same. Both are expensive. But the main message is that each option requires social controls of different kinds, and neither seems to reduce the need for strong central authority and planning.

With the nuclear future, central goverment would have to exert tight controls on industry and local authorities over the siting of plants, transmission lines and so on. In the solar options, over 60 per cent of supplies come from small tree plantations plus wastes from forestry and paper industries. In all it means devoting some 6–7 per cent of the total land area to energy production – roughly the same as now used for agriculture. There would also be extensive use of wind machines – some 3,700 largish 4-megawatt units – solar electric cells (50 square metres per person), and communal solar district heating with large underground heat storage systems. Local authorities will need greatly increased powers and planning rights over small-scale energy producers and on siting decisions, while central government will have to play a strong directing and co-ordinating role.

As with the nuclear option, there are major technical uncertainties which can only be resolved through extensive and time-consuming research and development before any major commitment can be made to the all-solar future. Among the largest uncertainties are the environmental impacts of energy plantations or other biomass supplies, including nutrient leaching, insect attack, disease and land-use competition. Since these may be critical problems for Third World renewable energy futures, I shall return to them later.

Another message from this and other studies bears directly on the scale and control of renewable supplies. Nearly all soft-path sketches (see Figure 2) rely heavily on wind and hydro power to supply essential electricity needs. In Britain and a few other places one would include wave power, if the formidable engineering problems can be solved. For the quantities of energy we are talking about, these are emphatically not small-scale devices, nor can they be locally controlled. Because the winds (and waves) are unreliable, they must either be backed up by fuel-burning power stations or combined with hydro-electric schemes to provide energy storage in the lakes behind the dams. These problems of supply variation and storage call for large, extensive and perhaps international grid systems with sophisticated load-management centres to control them. Furthermore, all serious wind power enthusiasts today assume that for environmental reasons most of the wind generators will be bunched into large 'wind parks', preferably offshore and out of sight. Who is to manage all this: the friendly neighbourhood utility or the Central Electricity (By Any Means) Generating Board?

These requirements for large-scale systems, including international energy connections and trade, are now common features of any sophisticated soft-energy scenario. The ambitious 'soft-solar' scenario that Richard Caputo and Michael Messenger of the International Institute of Advanced Systems Analysis are now developing for Western Europe is an excellent example which is worth considering for a moment.

Dealing with 19 countries in an area from Norway to Spain and Ireland to Turkey, they have considered a nuclear scenario, a 'hard-solar' scenario based largely on centralized energy sources, and the 'soft-solar' scenario. In all cases there is a very strong emphasis on energy-saving and a sensible matching of energy types to end-use needs. They also assume some economic growth to provide for added employment and for relative poverty in the region. Consequently, energy demand increases in each scenario by 1.6 times over the next 50 to 100 years.

In the 'soft-solar' scenario the cardinal assumption is that desires for self-reliance and local autonomy lead to a system where energy is produced wherever possible at the point of use. Only if these ultra-decentralized supplies are inadequate are neighbourhood, village or district level systems used. These in turn are backed up only when needed by central sources at a national level and then by international energy transfers.

To achieve this maximally decentralized system some fairly heroic assumptions have to be made. For example, the entire roof and wall area of the building stock has to be used for solar heating, including 4,000 km^2 of solar cells for electricity generation. Electricity is also provided by 52,000 large 6-megawatt wind turbines in regional wind centres and about 1.4 million small 6-kilowatt turbines installed on farms and other rural buildings. Large, central solar installations covering 17,000 square kilometres of land provide back-up electricity and hydrogen as a storable, transportable fuel.

Plant or biomass sources contribute only 13 per cent of total energy. The scenario examines a variety of mixes: forestry, agricultural energy farms, urban and agricultural wastes, with various conversions to portable liquid fuels and direct use for burning. In these mixes, the total land area for biomass production ranges from 0.15 to 0.35 million km^2, or 3.4 per cent to 8 per cent of the region's total land area. The current combined area of all agricultural land and forests in the region is 3.6 million km^2, or roughly 10 to 20 times the amount to be devoted to energy production. However, most biomass production would have to be in the central latitudes, where just over 9 per cent of available land is for growing fuels.

Clearly, in this small-focussed future there would have to be vast movements of energy across regional and national borders. In fact, it turns out that only one quarter of all the solar energy can be provided at the most decentralized on-site level, with another 15 per cent provided at the district level. So 40 per cent of all energy supplies could be locally controlled. That leaves some 50 per cent of supplies to be produced at a national or regional level, mostly from large-scale units, with the remaining 10 per cent coming from international or intercontinental flows.

Although the balance in scale of energy systems is different from today's, it is very far from the utopian visions of the decentralist movement. Moreover, since no society can assume that such a future will come about, other moves will have to be started in the meantime to reduce our awesome dependence on OPEC oil and, in a decade or two, OPEC natural gas.

These moves need not be towards nuclear power. More probably there will be a vast increase in the production and international trade of coal, which is already beginning to get under way. Couple these essential insurance strategies with the news from this analysis that the ultra-soft path may not be so soft after all, and where stands the prevailing argument that choices of small versus big, self-reliance versus remote manipulation, should be the critical features in the design of our energy futures?

If this is true of industrialized countries, what of the Third World? Don't they present an even more compelling case for renewable energies, mostly on a small scale, as the swiftest and most appropriate path for development? Most of their populations live and farm in rural areas: they could grow fuels as well as food, or otherwise convert the bountiful sunshine of the tropical and sub-tropical belts. Most developing countries lack the large, conventional energy systems on which we rely, and the electricity grids, pipelines and roads to distribute energy, especially to rural areas. Many have no discovered fossil fuel resources of their own and must import most of their energy, sometimes at a crippling cost in foreign exchange. More than half of the Third World now relies on petroleum for at least 90 per cent of its commercial or 'modern' energy (coal, oil, gas, electricity), while total dependence on oil and gas – the hydrocarbon fuels nearest to depletion – is close to 80 per cent. As a result of all this, conventional energy, when it is available at all, is usually extremely expensive in rural areas, even by our standards of income. Prices for electricity, paraffin (kerosene) for cooking and lighting, or diesel fuel for tractors, irrigation pumps and generators, are normally several, and sometimes as much as ten, times those in developed countries.

Last, but by no means least, is the firewood crisis. In many rural areas, firewood used mainly for cooking, or to provide charcoal to feed the cooking stoves of the towns and cities, is rapidly depleting. In the arid or semi-arid regions of Africa and Asia the land within 100 kilometres of some cities has been stripped of firewood trees, repeating a process that occurred centuries ago in the great historic settlement regions of China, central and northern India, and the deltas of the Ganges and the Nile.

Anything that can be done to relieve these stresses and increase, for many purposes, the energy available to the developing world is clearly worth doing. But how much can we realistically expect from renewable energies; and on what scale should they best be provided? The answers are not as clear cut as many people now appear to believe.

If we start with the most immediate point of strain – the provision of cooking fuel – it is now increasingly clear that an almost infinitely decentralized approach, finely tuned to the needs and perceptions of people, is essential.

The reason is that for the great majority of villagers, (who use firewood, or dung and crop wastes) their principal fuels are what the economists call 'free goods'. Their collection imposes not monetary but social costs which bring certain social benefits. Furthermore, these costs and benefits are only parts of a complex network of costs, benefits and trade-offs that are between them the heart of village life. Thus to the villager it may not seem nearly as obvious as it does to the passing expert that there is a fuelwood problem at all, let alone that he – or usually she – should save time collecting wood by spending time planting and caring for trees, or should give up an 'inefficient' open cooking fire which will burn any combustible material for an 'efficient' stove that can only burn sticks of a prescribed size.

My colleagues Gerald Foley and Ariane van Buren have spent much of the past two years exploring these issues on the ground in China, Tanzania and Senegal, and have come to some disturbing conclusions. The first is that there are very few existing alternatives to fuelwood, whether substitute-fuels, technologies or other remedial measures, that are sufficiently sensitive to these social factors to be accepted as appropriate. The estimated 7 million biogas plants in China are a rare exception based on an existing tradition of intensive animal rearing and manuring that is hardly found elsewhere. Yet only when the 'solution' is seen by the people themselves to match their totality of problems can outsiders help devise ways for people to improve their lot.

This point is widely recognized in discussions on appropriate technology. But my colleagues go further. Because in most subsistence societies there are many scarcities and priorities in village life, recognition that energy supply is the priority demanding action will come only when the free-good fuels have gone far towards total depletion. In many parts of semi-arid Africa, women and children now spend several hours a day collecting firewood, yet the highest family and village priorities still lie elsewhere – in building mud brick houses, perhaps, or better transport, water supply and sanitation.

Consequently, none of the many solutions so often advocated seem capable of preventing the widespread depletion of fuelwood. In many parts of the world 'an inevitable progression seems to be taking place towards a state in which the freely available wood resource, on which rural areas totally rely and from which much of the charcoal for the cities is made, will no longer be able to meet the demands placed upon it.'

If my colleagues are right, then radical preventative measures will be needed, few of them fitting easily with 'appropriate development'. One is to bring fuelwood and charcoal into the cash economy. If villagers must pay for fuel and can also sell it on to the towns and cities as wood or charcoal, there could be strong pressures to expand resources by planting trees and to conserve what there is by more careful, efficient use. There are several means of doing this, while the cash sales would also provide village incomes to invest in them.

Another approach is to start fairly large-scale plantations of fast-growing trees. These are often glibly advocated as a medium- and long-term answer for mass energy production in the Third World to provide not only firewood and charcoal but also, through various conversion methods, portable and cheaply transportable liquid fuels such as methanol. Similar claims are made for 'energy farming' of sugar cane, cassava and other crops that can be converted to versatile liquid fuels such as ethanol.

But how appropriate – or even how renewable – are these biomass sources? For a start, they clearly involve some fairly profound changes in farming and thus in village life, through a change in scale and centralization. Sugar cane cannot be grown and processed economically except on a scale of tens or usually hundreds of acres. Cassava is normally a garden crop. Will farmers accept, and with what penalties in freedom, the move from small-scale food growing to large-scale energy cash cropping or forestry? Experience from the

Brazilian alcohol-from-biomass programme has hardly been encouraging, although of course it would be foolish to assert that satisfactory solutions cannot be found.

Equally worrying are some of the environmental and ecological implications. In virtually every present method of biomass energy production, all the plant material is removed and converted to fuels or animal-feed residues that are too valuable to return to the land. (The single, notable exception is again biogas production; in China the nitrogen-rich fertilizer residue is considered a more important by-product than the gas itself.) Synthetic fertilizers can replace some of the nutrient losses, but add considerably to money and energy costs. The loss of most or all of the plant material that is normally recycled to maintain soil structure and fertility is potentially far more serious. Several studies have recently established that if husbanding the soil is given high priority, the potential for net production of biomass energy from each acre of land is drastically reduced. Using this criterion, Pimentel has estimated that the total energy from biomass that can safely be harvested from the vast acreages of the USA is only 2 per cent of present energy consumption.

Vaclav Smil comes to a similar conclusion for the most densely populated tropical regions, where pressures on land make crop by-products the only realistic biomass energy source. These by-products, Smil argues, have indispensable alternative uses and are not – nor should become – available for energy production. In the lowlands of China and India, for example, where fodder crops are virtually non-existent and draft animals provide most of the motive power, nearly three-quarters of all harvested straws, stalks and leaves are used as animal feed or bedding.

Even in low-density regions, and neglecting all issues of soil health, competition between food and fuels for land and water raises serious doubts on the large-scale availability of energy from biomass resources. An excellent illustration is the largest existing experiment of this kind: the Brazilian National Alcohol Programme. In 1979 it provided 3 billion litres of alcohol using sugar cane and cassava because of their high energy yields from each planted acre. The average gross energy yield was close to four barrels of oil-equivalent per acre, but allowing for the high-grade energy used to grow and process the crops the net yield would have been much less – and by some calculations zero. By 1985, Brazil expects to more than double this production with 5 to 7 million acres planted to cane and cassava. This should provide one fiftieth of the country's oil consumption on a tenth of its present total cropped area. Meanwhile the USA plans by the same date to produce alcohol from 800 million bushels of corn grown on 8 million acres released from its 'land bank'. The USA currently supplies four-fifths of the world's traded grain and the largest grain importer in the western hemisphere is Brazil.

Brazil and North America could, of course, expand their cultivated areas. Hopefully, species can be developed for marginal lands and deserts too dry for food production. The land resources that the North squanders through food extravagance and the South underuses through ignorance or lack of agricultural inputs could, if fairly distributed, banish hunger and provide copious fuels – or so the argument goes. Who knows what could happen to an idea so young? But what does seem clear from all the controversies surrounding energy from biomass is that for it to make a significant contribution to global energy needs we may have to move a very long way indeed from small-scale, decentralized and otherwise 'soft' methods and look to large-scale (although ecologically diverse) systems with management, distribution and trade on a national and international scale.

Similar conclusions apply to many other ways of providing energy for the Third World. The contentious issue of rural electrification from central power stations by extending grid systems is now strongly challenged by hopes for scattered electrification based on small-scale, local renewable sources: wind generators, small hydro-power, solar cells and generators run on gasifying various crop wastes.

I am sure that all these approaches will have some place, somewhere. What disturbs me is the chorus of assertions that because grid electrification has often been slow and costly, the small renewable systems are generally going to be quicker and cheaper to put in place.

I am unhappily convinced that most small, renewable sources will be extremely costly either in human skills and time or in capital investments. With most of the renewables one has to establish, place by place, not only the energy and cultural appropriateness of the technology but also the local resource endowments. How often here – not in the next valley or the weather station 100 kilometres away – does the wind blow and how strongly? How does one provide energy storage to smooth out the wind's irregularities, or a back-up system when it fails for long periods? What will that cost? Enormous efforts of data gathering, experiment, adaptation, trials, demonstration and diffusion both of successes and failures will be needed.

In contrast, the development of conventional energy systems seems relatively easy; and for the next decade or two, more urgent. Many developing countries are stressed close to the point of breakdown by the direct impact of high oil prices and their indirect effects on worldwide recession, inflation and worsening terms of trade. Their agriculture and industries must be kept running, let alone improved. By whatever means this is done, renewable energies have virtually nothing to offer yet. Furthermore, most Third World countries have extremely limited human resources for planning their existing energy systems. What strengths they have lie in the energy systems they have come to rely on over the past three decades: oil, hydropower, electricity grids, and in some cases coal and natural gas. There is little capacity, if any, to spare for possibly slow and risky innovations except where crisis is imminent, as in fuelwood and charcoal supplies in many places.

Given these conditions, surviving the next decade or two will and should be the main priorities of energy policy. Sustainability over the medium term must always be a more important criterion than long-run renewability.

One must also recognize that there are the fuels and the international mechanisms to provide this sustainability, so long as one discards the paradigm that only small is best or renewable beautiful. For example, more than half of the world's likely but unexplored oil-bearing sediments lie in oil-importing developing countries. The World Bank has estimated that 30 to 40 poor countries that do not now produce oil have the potential to do so economically. Large multilateral and bilateral funding programmes have now begun to produce this oil. There are enormous untapped hydropower resources in many Third World countries, but they are often on a scale too large for the owning country to develop or use: regional alliances and grid interconnections could tap these potentials. World Coal resources are enormous. At an average production and shipping cost of around $40–60 per tonne, coal is now 3 to 4 times cheaper than oil at $35 a barrel. The developed countries are gearing rapidly to produce, trade and use this coal; can developing countries be helped to get in on the act with assistance in building terminals to land, store and distribute coal, the knowledge and technologies to use it? For most large-scale uses in industry and for power generation coal can replace oil – and it is conceivable even as a fuel for the villages. Several studies on the feasibility of replacing fuelwood and charcoal by coal are now in progress, while the Chinese have been cooking with it for decades.

I do not imagine that any of these routes to the energy future will be straight or smooth. All I have tried to suggest here is that for many reasons they should not be rejected simply for the sake of an alternative vision of how things could be. Soft-energy futures are also difficult and may have their disappointments.

As Hazel Henderson has put it in another context: we have to go beyond either/or; it's going to be both/and. I am also sure that Fritz Schumacher would have agreed. In *Small is Beautiful*, he carefully argued that there is no single answer to the question of what scale is appropriate. For different purposes people need different structures, both small ones and large ones, yet often find it difficult to keep these two seemingly opposite necessities in mind. They always tend to clamour for a final solution. He then added, significantly: 'Today we suffer from an almost universal idolatry of giantism. It is therefore necessary to insist on the virtues of smallness – where this applies. If there were a prevailing idolatry of smallness . . . one would have to try and exercise influence in the opposite direction.' That is all I have tried to do.

IV

Peak Experience*

Colin Wilson

I was going to write a book about Schumacher just before he died – I feel that his ideas were a natural extension, in a social direction, of my own work.

I had always been preoccupied with the problem of the person who stands alone in a society that he feels to be too big and too impersonal. This was the basic theme of *The Outsider*.

Somewhere in *The Outsider* I say that I feel the Outsider dislikes the whole idea of civilization itself, because it destroys the sense of individuality. That is, of course, a deliberate overstatement. And yet, lecturing in America not long after *The Outsider* came out, I was struck by the awful impersonality of the universities, where in many cases the classes were so big that the students had to sit in other rooms watching the lecture on a TV monitor. I could see clearly that it must be almost impossible for many of these students to get that *personal*, individual feeling that could develop into creativity.

Because this, it seems to me is the fundamental aim of civilization. This is what it is about. It is an attempt to promote creativity in the individual, because this is the highest thing of which the individual is capable.

In the late 1950s, I received a letter from the Amer-

---

* This lecture was delivered impromptu, without notes, which may account for some of the shortcomings in its style.

ican psychologist Abraham Maslow, who was writing to me about a book of mine called *The Age of Defeat*. Maslow said that I was attacking the same problem that had obsessed him for years: that our civilization has a kind of *premise of defeat* – that our art, our literature, our culture seems to spring from the notion that ultimately the individual cannot make much of an impression on the civilization; he is helpless, a mere member of the crowd.

Maslow also sent me some of his papers. I must admit that when I read their rather academic titles, I delayed reading them for a long time. When I did start to read one of the papers, about six months later, I was immediately excited by Maslow's central thesis, which was this: that psychologists are always studying sick people, because sick people are always talking about their sickness, while nobody had ever thought of studying healthy people, because healthy people never talk about their health. Maslow argued that we would do better to study the healthy. He enquired among his friends, asking, 'Who is the healthiest person you know?' And then he proceeded to study a number of these healthy people, and was amazed to discover something that no one had ever discovered before, because no one had ever thought of studying healthy people: that is, most of them appeared to experience with a fair degree of frequency what Maslow called 'peak experiences'. These were just sudden bubbling, overwhelming moments of happiness. They were not in any sense *mystical* experiences. A young mother was watching her husband and kids eating breakfast, when suddenly a beam of sunlight came in through the window, and she thought, 'Aren't I lucky', and went into the peak experience. A hostess who had just given a very successful party, looking around the room at the cigarette butts trampled into the carpet, and the wine spilled on the armchairs, nevertheless suddenly went into the peak experience. Maslow said that the peak experience seemed to characterize all healthy people. It was basically a sudden powerful surge of unconscious vitality. I was immensely struck by this, and wrote to Maslow about it. I ended by writing a book about him called *New Pathways in Psychology*.

As soon as I read Schumacher's *Small is Beautiful*, I could see that this was a logical extension of Maslow's ideas – that the healthy person is the person who does not feel overwhelmed by his environment. He doesn't feel helpless, he doesn't feel a cog in a machine; he preserves a sense of drive, of individuality and creativity. And clearly the problem for the whole civilization is this problem of how to keep things 'small' enough, so that as many people as possible can experience the sense of individuality.

I recognized that my own background in Leicester, my home town, had exercised a strong influence on me, largely because it was so claustrophobic and boring. And the same appears to be true of an enormous amount of writers of the present century: James Joyce's Dublin, Bernard Shaw's Dublin, H. G. Wells's Lewisham, Arnold Bennett's Burslem, Proust's Combray – all very small places that enable their inhabitants to feel individual among other individuals. Of course, what it really amounts to is feeling yourself to be a small fish in a small pond. If you are a small fish in a big pond, you are bound to lack that sense of individuality. I recognized this when I first went to London at about the age of nineteen: the feeling of being completely lost in crowds – that if I was knocked down by a bus, nobody would care. Obviously, we all crave this sense of individuality. Now Maslow had recognized that human beings appear to evolve through a series of needs, or values; he called it 'the hierarchy of needs.'

What he meant was this: that if a person was starving and had never had a square meal in his life, then he would dream about food and imagine that perfect happiness would be to have one really good meal every day. Yet if he achieved this, the next level would emerge: the need for security, for a roof over one's head. (This is why every tramp daydreams of a country cottage with roses round the door.) If he achieves this 'territorial' level, then the next level emerges: the need for love, for a feeling of belongingness, of intimacy with another person or persons. If these needs are satisfied too, says Maslow, then the next level emerges: the need for self-esteem, the need to be respected and liked by other people. This is the level at which women invite the neighbours to coffee mornings, and men join Rotary Clubs.

If the self-esteem level is thoroughly satisfied, then, said Maslow, the next level — with luck — emerges (and he said 'with luck' because, for some reason, many people do not appear to ever reach this level): this is the creative level, what Maslow called 'self-actualization'. By this, he didn't necessarily mean art or science or some other form of creativity. Self-actualization means doing something purely for the pleasure of doing it well. In one case he cited, a woman was particularly good at fostering children, and continued to do this when her own children were grown up. Another man was skilful at putting ships in bottles, and he did it brilliantly: obviously, this satisfied the self-actualizing need in him. Self-actualization seems to be the pinnacle of the hierarchy of needs.

Fortunately, in our society, most people have achieved the first three levels anyway – the basic needs for food, for security and for some kind of warm human relationship. The need that a majority of people have still not satisfied, and that becomes increasingly urgent in a society like ours, is the self-esteem need – the need, if you like, for some kind of 'recognition', if only by a very small group of neighbours and friends. And this is obviously one of the basic problems of our civilization, with its increasing tendency to de-individuation: self-esteem. It obviously cannot be satisfied if you are in such an enormous pond that you feel alienated from everybody else – in other words, if you feel a nobody.

This is what I identified in *The Outsider* as the basic Outsider problem. Now, it seemed to me that in recognizing that it *is* possible to decentralize society, to live in much smaller units, Schumacher had made an immensely important contribution. He had, of course, been anticipated by idealists like G. K. Chesterton and Hilaire Belloc, who called their political philosophy 'Distributism'; it was usually summarized in the phrase, 'Two acres and a cow.' Clearly, two acres and a cow would not solve the problems of the modern city-dweller. But Schumacher had seen that Distributism *could* be brought up to date – that we could live in a completely different kind of way. When I first came upon his ideas – in a television programme – they excited me so much because it was already clear to me that we have *got* to live in a completely different kind of way if we are to satisfy the basic human need for self-esteem. And, as Maslow said, unless we satisfy this need for self-esteem, it is impossible to move beyond it to the level of self-actualization – which would be the ideal level for society.

I wrote to Schumacher; we corresponded, and I went to see him at his home to discuss the idea of a book about him. (He was also a friend of Maslow.) Then, while the book was still in the planning stage, he died. It was only after *Guide for the Perplexed* came out that I realized that Schumacher, like myself, had turned away from the social aspect of the problem – which is indeed very important – towards what seems to me to be in a sense even more important: the problem of the lone individual in our society.

At the time when I wrote *The Outsider* – in my early 20s – I was hardly interested in politics, and after every lecture I gave, somebody would always ask the same question: 'This is all very well, but how could your ideas improve our society?' And I always had to admit that I couldn't see any obvious way in which they would improve our social conditions. For, as far as I could see, improving society has to start by improving the individual. It was pleasant for me to discover that this was the conclusion Schumacher came to in *Guide for the Perplexed*. And in that beautiful appendix – for anyone who hasn't read the book, I suggest you start with the epilogue – he quotes Dorothy L. Sayers on the subject of Dante; she said that Dante's *Inferno* is a picture of human society in a state of sin and corruption, and then goes on to say that these are the problems of our own society: 'Futility, lack of a living faith, drift into loose morality, greedy consumption, financial irresponsibility, self-opinionated and obstinate individualism, and violence.' Schumacher goes on to point out that Dorothy L. Sayers wrote this 30 years ago, and that things, if anything, are now much worse. Then he goes on to say that the real problem is that we are trying to live without a religion – and I don't think for a moment that Schumacher meant a religion in the sense of some religious sect. What he meant was the kind of inner certainty which provides an anchor against the sense of alienation.

Even at the time I wrote *The Outsider*, I could see that this was the central problem. If you had an absolutely ideal society with enough material goods for everybody, it would obviously still not guarantee universal happiness. In point of fact, as a student of crime – I am writing *A Criminal History of Mankind* at the moment – I have always recognized that one of the worst consequences of an increasingly comfortable civilization is a soaring crime rate. What is worse still is that the crimes become increasingly violent and sadistic. There are certain crimes of the past two decades – particularly certain examples of mass murder – that would simply never have happened before the 1960s. There has been an increase in deliberate sadism that is obviously due to sheer frustration.

Yes, the problem begins with the individual, because in an ideal society you could still not guarantee an end to all crimes of frustration. It is obviously necessary, as Schumacher says, to think in terms of religion. Bernard Shaw was one of the first people to recognize this clearly, and to state, 'Modern man cannot live without a religion.' Arnold Toynbee made this one of the central theses in *A Study of History*. And Schumacher is the third important thinker of this century to put his finger on this basic problem.

Now religion is fundamentally something that you live by. Whitehead once said, 'Religion is what a man does with his solitude.' Religion is also the ability to induce in oneself a certain inner peace. For me, one of the most important sections in *The Outsider* deals with the novelist Herman Hesse. (In fact, I was the first person to write about him extensively in English.) I was particularly excited by his novel *Steppenwolf*, which seemed to me to express this central problem with unparalleled clarity. Steppenwolf is a would-be writer who is fairly well-off; he lives in a comfortable room in a comfortable lodging house; he has plenty of books and gramophone records; he has a girlfriend; in fact, he seems to have most of the things that a human being needs to be happy. And yet, for some reason,

Steppenwolf is not happy. His problem is a continual feeling of boredom and frustration, that inability to break through to forms of deeper mental intensity. He feels that his consciousness is somehow boring and lukewarm. In the early pages of the book, he describes his frustration and the occasional temptation to commit suicide. Then, later that day, he wanders along to a restaurant for a meal, and as he tastes his first glass of Moselle he experiences that curious sense of deep relaxation that Maslow calls the peak experience. He says, 'The golden bubble burst and I was reminded of Mozart and the stars.'

And this goes to the heart of the matter. If *only* there were a way in which you could push a button and induce that experience instantly – make the golden bubble burst so that you are reminded of Mozart and the stars. If only we could do that – if we could even find some drug or chemical that would do it – then we would have solved the basic problem of modern civilization. No more crime, no more war, no more frustration and hatred. Aldous Huxley, you may remember, even suggested that we should all take mescalin for that purpose; but the trouble with mescalin is that it makes you so ecstatically lazy and happy that you don't want to do anything at all. A pile of unwashed dishes looks so beautiful that nobody would ever want to wash them. So clearly, this is not the answer. Yet you can see that, if we could find a method of inducing Maslow's peak experience at will, we *would* have found the answer to this problem.

Schumacher makes another point of fundamental importance in *Guide for the Perplexed*, in the section called 'Adaequatio': that the problem is that the information that comes in through our senses is *not* reality. He points out that we see not only with our eyes, but with a great part of our mental equipment as well. And since this mental equipment varies greatly from person to person, there are inevitably many things some people can see while others can't. 'Or to put it differently, for which some people are adequate while others are not. When the level of the knower is not adequate to the level of the object of knowledge, the result is not factual error but something much more serious: an inadequate and impoverished view of reality.' Now there, it seems to me, Schumacher has gone to the very heart of the fundamental problem of human existence.

This problem has to do with our senses, and with the curiously 'impoverished view of reality' that we hold. And this, I could see from my *Outsider* days, was the heart of the problem. Steppenwolf solves it for a moment by taking a drink of Moselle, but wine doesn't always work, and if you rely upon it you become an alcoholic. Wine, mescalin, pot – all these chemical ways of solving the problem tend to let us down half the time. This was something Maslow discovered when he and a psychologist called Hoffer were treating alcoholics. Maslow concluded that alcoholics are very often more intelligent than the average person, and consequently they find the world more dreary and boring than most people; like Wordsworth, they find that 'the world is too much with them'. They drink because drinking gives them a brief peak experience, but it doesn't always work. Sometimes you can feel completely ecstatic on a glass of wine or beer; at other times you can drink a whole bottle of gin and still feel depressed. The alcoholic nevertheless keeps on drinking because this to him seems to be the only way back to the peak experience. And, of course, as they become more resistant to the alcohol, they need larger quantities, and the problem is complicated by a feeling of guilt . . .

Now Maslow started from the assumption that the

alcoholic was probably more intelligent than the average person. He would ask, 'What kind of things gave you a peak experience before you became an alcoholic?' Some would mention visual things – paintings, beautiful scenery; others, poetry, music, ballet. What Maslow and Hoffer then did was to administer a psychedelic drug which produced a kind of artificial 'lift', and then would induce intense peak experiences by means of colours blending on a screen, music, poetry read aloud, and so on. They discovered that they got something like an 85 per cent permanent cure rate. Why? Because the alcoholic was like a man on a kind of descending escalator, doing his best to induce peak experiences but remaining essentially passive, allowing the will to remain half-asleep – waiting, in other words, for the alcohol to carry him like a magic carpet into the peak experience. But as soon as he was carried into a far more intense peak experience by the mescalin and poetry, he would recognize clearly that the peak experience depends upon *health*, and that health in turn depends upon a powerful will-drive. Just as the body feels healthiest when you are taking plenty of exercise, so the emotions feel healthiest when the will is well exercised. And as soon as the alcoholic recognized this, he instantly ceased to be an alcoholic. In a sense you could say that he changed drugs, and used will instead of alcohol. Now this seems to me to be getting very close to a solution of the problem of 'impoverished reality'.

Graham Greene stumbled upon another clue, which he describes in an essay called *The Revolver in the Corner Cupboard*. He describes how, in his teens, his schoolmasters became alarmed because he appeared to dislike sport and sent him to a psychiatrist. After six months of analysis, Greene was much better 'socially adjusted', but found that he was in a state of total depression. He said that everything he looked at appeared to be grey and dull. He could look at some scene which he saw *visually* to be beautiful but about which he felt nothing whatever. He was in this state of inner-deadness when he discovered in a corner cupboard a revolver belonging to his older brother. He took this on to Berkhamsted Common and played Russian roulette – put one bullet in the chambers, pointed it at his head and pulled the trigger. When there was just a click, he looked down the barrel and saw that the bullet had now come into position. So he had missed death by just one chamber. He said that he instantly experienced an overwhelming feeling of ecstasy and happiness. He said, 'It was as if a light had been turned on and I suddenly saw that life is infinitely beautiful'.

I was excited by this story, when I came across it in my early teens, because it shows so clearly what goes wrong with us. When we are bored and tired we are, so to speak, 'spread out'; the will is slack; you are passive, like an exhausted swimmer lying on a beach. The moment Greene pointed the gun at his head and pulled the trigger, he went into violent tension. And when he heard the click, he relaxed. And *that* is the essence of the peak experience. It is a tensing of the will, followed by total relaxation. A movement of contraction followed by expansion. Moreover, the relaxation doesn't work unless you become tense first. It is like those handbrakes on old cars, where you have to pull it towards you and tighten it before it can be released.

Using Greene's insight, I evolved a technique for inducing peak experiences. What I did was this: I would take a pencil and hold it up against a blank wall. I would concentrate intently on the pencil until I saw nothing but the pencil; then I'd let go completely, until

I could see the whole background of the wall behind the pencil. Then I would concentrate intently on the pencil again, and then let go again, and so on. When I had done that about ten times, I would begin to feel a kind of pain behind the eyes. When you feel that pain, press on as hard as you can, because you are almost there. Two or three more times and suddenly you relax totally into the peak experience. And if you do it with total conviction, it always works. Not long ago in Finland, I was explaining this technique to a class, and in the following session I explained to them about Wilhelm Reich's breathing techniques. Reich said that in order to breathe properly you must take a deep breath, then allow it to go out first of all from the chest, then from the stomach, and then finally from the genitals. As Reich made his patients do this, he would say, 'Out, down, through.' I was explaining the Reichian breathing to them as we all lay around on the floor and then, on the spur of the moment, I decided to try and combine it with the 'pencil trick'. Breathing slowly and deeply, we held the pencil up against the ceiling, concentrated intently, and then let go. To my astonishment, the two combined perfectly. Within a few minutes, I felt almost as if I had floated up from the floor towards the ceiling. The curious thing is that the total concentration of the pencil exercise and the total relaxation of the breathing exercise somehow combine in the most peculiar way to produce an instant peak experience. We all lay there quietly for well over half an hour, until I looked at my watch and said, 'Hey! We are missing lunch!'

But why does it work? I discovered the answer only a few years ago, when I was reading a book about the split-brain experiments of Roger Sperry and Michael Gazzaniga. I must admit it came to me as a revelation.

What it amounts to is this. If you could take off the

top of your head and look down on the brain, it would look like a walnut joined together by a kind of bridge. This bridge is called the *corpus callosum*, or commissure – a block of nerve fibres. In the 1930s it was discovered that severing the commissure would prevent epileptic attacks: it appears to prevent the electrical storm from passing from one side of the brain to the other. Oddly enough, this operation appeared to make no difference whatever to the patient. No one could quite understand why this should be so. Somebody even suggested that the only purpose of the *corpus callosum* is to stop the brain from sagging in the middle. It wasn't until Roger Sperry began repeating these experiments in the 1950s that he discovered that, in fact, there *is* a basic difference in split-brain patients. The difference is that you become two people.

We have known for about a century that the left side of the brain deals with speech, reason, coping with the external world. The right side of the brain deals with pattern recognition and intuition. To put it crudely, the left side is a scientist and the right an artist. For some odd reason, the left side of the brain controls the right side of the body and vice versa – no one knows why. We could also say – I am deliberately over-simplifying – that the left cerebral hemisphere controls the right eye and the right hemisphere controls the left eye. Now if you show a split-brain patient an apple with the left eye and an orange with the right – so that one cannot see what the other is looking at – and ask, 'What have I just shown you?', he will reply, 'An orange'. But if you say, 'Write with your left hand what I have just shown you', he will write, 'Apple.' And if you say, 'What have you just written?', he would reply, 'Apple.' In the same way, a patient who was shown a dirty picture with the right side of her brain blushed. When asked why she was blushing, she said, 'I don't know.'

One split-brain patient tried to embrace his wife with his right hand while the left tried to push her away. Another tried to do up his flies with his right hand – connected to the logical half of the brain – while the left tried to undo them. Obviously, the two different sides of the brain had completely different intentions.

Now you observe that when the patient is asked, 'What have *you* seen?', it is the left side of the brain that answers the question. In other words, the person you call 'you' lives in the left side of your head. The person who lives over there in the right-hand side is a total stranger. Now you will say that this is obviously untrue because *we* are not split-brain patients. Yet, in an important sense, we are. Mozart said, for example, that melodies were always walking straight into his head fully formed. What he meant was: melodies were walking out of his right brain into the part of the brain in which *he* lived. And this is true for all of us. Although we are vaguely aware of the right brain and its activities, we are not closely *connected* to it. This explains, for example, why you become self-conscious if someone looks over your shoulder when you are writing. When you are engaged in any interesting task, you 'forget yourself' and become absorbed in what you are doing. The left and right brain enter into close collaboration, the right supplying the intuition, the left supplying the mechanical skills. When someone looks over your shoulder, the left becomes 'self-conscious' and promptly loses contact with the right. The flow of meaning stops, and you feel somehow 'stranded' in the present moment. The same thing would happen if you tried to play a piano attending *to* your fingers. You would play very badly indeed. A good pianist ignores his fingers – he attends *from* the fingers to the music. Attending *to* things is a sure way of screwing yourself up. You must attend *from* them to the meaning.

I could recognize the same process in my activity as a writer. When I first started writing, I found that trying to capture intuitions on paper seemed to strangle the life out of them. When I went back to look at what I'd written the next morning, it wasn't there anymore. The words seemed dead and lifeless. The meaning had evaporated. I even began to suspect that words are a straightjacket that cripple the intuitions. But I kept on trying, because that was all there was to do, and eventually I found that I got good at it. One day, I re-read what I'd written the night before, and it was still there. And after that, I recognized that good writing was an interplay between two halves of the brain, very much like a game of tennis. The right produces the insights and the left turns them into words. If the left verbalizes an insight with particular neatness, the right gets excited and says, 'Yes, yes, that's exactly what I meant!' And the left would say, 'Really? Thank you', and would proceed to do it even better. And then suddenly the two of them were working together like a couple of top-class tennis players, or like two lumberjacks at either end of a double-handled saw. States like this are obviously what we call inspiration – and they consist of perfect co-operation between the right and the left.

Another interesting thing discovered by Sperry is that the left brain works much quicker than the right. The left is the go-getter. It is turned towards the external world: it copes with reality. The right, on the other hand, appears to be turned inwards, towards our inner world. Its business is to supply us with energy, with strength and purpose; hence, of course, the peak experience.

But because the left is fast and the right is slow, they find some difficulty in reaching a state of empathy. This explains why the peak experiences are relatively rare. The right saunters along slowly with its hands in its pockets; the left walks with a kind of nervous haste. The result is that there is soon a large gap between them and they can no longer hear one another. There seem to be two ways of getting the two halves to work at the same speed. One is to make the left go slower, the other is to make the right go faster. We can make the left go slower by meditation and relaxation. We can make the right go faster by deliberately working ourselves into a state of excitement – this is the aim of African drumming or the repetitious beat of pop music.

Now when this happens you can compare the situation to two trains running on parallel tracks that are suddenly running side by side, so that the people can lean out of the windows and talk to one another. Here you can see we are beginning to grasp the mechanics of the peak experience.

Our basic problem, as you can see, is that the 'you' who lives in the left side of the brain is not even aware that it has this immensely powerful co-worker. You notice this particularly when you feel tense and anxious: the more anxious you become, the more the 'you' tends to take over, and the more it becomes separated from the source of power in the right brain. The more anxious we become, the weaker we become. You can see why I say that we are, in a factual sense, all split-brain patients. In the peak experiences, or those curious moments of total happiness and relaxation, we simply recognize that we have a powerful supporter, a companion who can take half the work from our shoulders.

For here is the important point: the right half of the brain is the creator of energy. He is the one who keeps us supplied with energy and vitality. You could compare the left and right halves to Laurel and Hardy in the old films. The left brain is Ollie, the fat one and the leader of the two. The right brain is much more

77

vague and easy-going – that's Stan. When you wake up on a dull Monday morning, 'you' wake up – that is, Ollie wakes up – and he looks out of the window and thinks, 'Oh God, it's Monday and it's raining . . .' Stan overhears him and Stan is, unfortunately, immensely *suggestible*. So he promptly sinks into depression. 'Oh God, it's *Monday* and it's *raining* . . .' For the trouble with Stan is that he is inclined to over-react. When Ollie is cheerful, Stan is delighted, when Ollie is gloomy, Stan is almost suicidal. But since Stan is in charge of the energy supply, he stops sending up energy when he feels depressed. So when Ollie goes down to breakfast, he feels curiously low and depressed. So he cuts himself while shaving, and trips on the pavement and drops his umbrella, and thinks, 'This is just one of those days when everything goes wrong . . .' And again Stan overhears him and plunges into even deeper gloom. In short, you will have what you might call a negative feedback situation, in which the misery of one keeps reinforcing the misery of the other.

Conversely, when a child wakes up on Christmas morning, his 'Ollie' says, 'Marvellous, it's Christmas!' And from then on, everything reinforces his feeling of delight and optimism: the decorations on the Christmas tree, the smell of cooking, the Christmas music on the radio . . . And both Stan and Ollie finally relax into such a state of trustful happiness that life seems totally transformed. Suddenly, everything is marvellous, and all the problems of yesterday appear trivial and quite unimportant. If we could cling on to this state of mind, human beings would become gods within the next century. And the key undoubtedly lies in the 'feedback mechanism' between Stan and Ollie.

Of course, it is true that there are drugs that will induce this state of intensified consciousness: Thomas De Quincey did it with laudanum. Yet neither alcohol nor drugs are a solution. Their basic effect is to produce a kind of animal consciousness. If you could get inside the skin of a cow or a dog, you would feel just as if you'd had three or four large whiskies. The world would seem pleasantly warm and real. They probably experience permanently the state that we experience only occasionally on beautifully spring mornings. You could say that animals are permanently drunk.

This, incidentally, could be the reason that animals appear to have certain paranormal powers – for example, second-sight. The wife of the Scottish poet Hugh McDiarmid told me that she always knew when he was coming back from a long journey because the dog would go and sit at the end of the lane waiting for him a couple of days before he arrived. Human beings can also achieve these powers when they relax completely; I have noticed this again and again in myself. I am totally ESP-thick until I am either very relaxed or very excited, and when that happens, the two halves are obviously in collaboration and my right begins to tell me the answers. Three or four years ago, I discovered to my astonishment that I could dowse. When a friend offered me a dowsing rod, I told him these things never work for me. He asked me to show him how I held it, and then said, 'You are holding it the wrong way. Twist the two ends in your hands so that there's a spring on the rod.' I did what he said, and walked towards a standing stone in the circle called the Merry Maidens. To my astonishment, the rod suddenly shot up. I was convinced that I had done it accidentally by twisting it, so I walked towards the next one – and it shot up again. Every time I went between the standing stones the dowsing rod twisted in my hands. It was quite obvious that something inside me was reacting to something in the ground or in the stones, but I, who live in my left brain, could feel nothing whatever. What was happening, I suspect, was that my muscles were tensing unconsciously – the striped muscles that are in the control of the right brain. The message was coming from the standing stones into my right brain, and the right brain was telling me that I was near something interesting by causing my muscles to convulse.

This seems to be confirmed by an experiment devised by Sperry. He tried flashing red and green lights at random into the blind eye – the left eye – of split-brain patients, and would ask, 'What colour have you just seen?' Of course, the split-brain patient had no idea. But if he was allowed a second guess he would always get it right, because if he said 'red' and the colour was actually green, he'd convulse as if someone had kicked him under the table. The right brain had heard the wrong guess, and was telling him so by making his muscles convulse – as in dowsing.

All this is to say that we have inside us – as Plato declared – a being who knows far more than *we* do, and who is perfectly willing to tell us. He is also perfectly willing to send us up any amount of energy; for where energy is concerned, he is the quartermaster whose job is to keep us supplied. Then why doesn't he always do so? Because, more often than not, the telephone line between the two halves is out of order. Tension isolates us in the left brain and separates us from the other half.

There is, of course, another side to this problem. When a man is drunk, he cannot insert the key into the keyhole. He is in a pleasant state of right-brain relaxation – he may even have a beautiful bird's-eye view of the universe – but his ability to concentrate microscopically on details no longer works. We can pay for right-brain relaxation with a certain loss of precision and accuracy, just as we pay for left-brain precision with a loss of right-brain relaxation. It is as if all of us had a telescope attached to one eye and a microscope to the other – the aim being to see into the distance and to be able to study things close-up. But when you look through a microscope, you close one eye. We tend to go around with one eye permanently closed, so we lose our distance-vision. Life becomes a kind of permanent worm's-eye view, an endless, boring close-upness, as unsatisfactory as going into a picture gallery and being forced to peer at all the pictures with your nose only an inch from the canvas. It is only in those curious moments of peak experience that we open both eyes and suddenly can see into the distance as well as what it is in front of our noses. On these occasions, we see the near and the far simultaneously.

L. H. Myers wrote a novel called *The Near and the Far* which expresses this very precisely. At the beginning of the novel, the young Prince Jali has travelled over the desert with his father to some congress of princes called by Akbar the Great. Standing on the battlements of Akbar's castle, he looks out over the desert and thinks, 'What a pity that the desert *looks* so beautiful and feels so exhausting to walk over.' It is as if there were two deserts, one of which is a glory to the eye and the other one a weariness to the foot. Isn't it a pity that we are unable to grasp the mystery and delight of the 'far'? Unfortunately, if you tried to grasp the ecstasy of the distance by rushing downstairs and out of doors, you would just get your shoes full of sand. It appears, Myers said, to be impossible to reconcile the near and the far.

Well, we can see that it is not. This is what the two halves of the brain were *intended* to do. When they work together, we can grasp the near and the far simultaneously.

They have another purpose which is even more interesting. In a book called *The Occult*, I wrote about what I called 'Faculty X'. In his *Study of History*, Arnold Toynbee described the experience that led him to begin writing the book. He had been climbing Mount Taygetus in Greece, and was sitting on the ruined walls of the citadel of Mystra, staring out over the plain of Sparta, when suddenly it struck him like a revelation that a few hundred years ago a hoard of barbarians had poured over that wall and destroyed the town, and that ever since then it had been a ruin. This realization was so powerful that he could almost see the barbarians clambering over the wall. Now this sudden curious sense of total reality is what I call Faculty X. Chesterton once said that we say thank you when someone passes us the salt, but we don't really *mean* it. We say the earth is round, but we don't really *mean* it, even though it is true. But when the astronauts went into space, they could say 'the earth is round' and *mean* it. That is Faculty X. When Proust tasted a biscuit dipped in tea, it filled him with a curious feeling of delight as it flooded him with memories of his childhood. He wrote, 'I had ceased to feel mediocre, accidental, mortal.' And when he tried to remember why it had caused him such pleasure, he recalled that when he was a child in Combray, his aunt had always given him a cake dipped in her herb tea when he went to see her, and this taste had suddenly revived the whole of his childhood. That is to say, a moment before he tasted the madeleine, he could *say*, 'Yes, I was a child in Combray', but he wouldn't have meant it. As soon as he tasted the madeleine he could taste it and *mean* it: Faculty X.

We can see what has happened. The unconscious part of the brain – and the right appears to be the gateway to the unconscious – has stored up memories of everything that has ever happened to us. But this library of tape recordings is not accessible to you unless you can relax sufficiently to somehow clear the telephone line. Or, to use my other analogy, get the two trains running at the same speed.

As absurd as it sounds, the reason we have two identical halves in the brain is so that we can be in two different places at the same time. We should be capable of being in the present *and somewhere else*. When we are stranded in the present, we lose all sense of perspective. We become lost in mere material reality. Our powers remain blocked and passive until we can achieve that double glimpse of the near and the far. In these moments we cease to be trapped in the worm's-eye view, and see the world simultaneously from a worm's-eye view and a bird's-eye view.

And because we are almost permanently trapped in a worm's-eye view, our instinctive feelings about the world tend to be negative. Normal consciousness can be compared to those nightmares when we try to run, but our legs seem too heavy. It is only in those moments of double-consciousness, the near and the far, that we seem to contact some source of power inside ourselves. Hence Proust's comment: 'I had ceased to feel mediocre, accidental, mortal.' *The underpinning of everyday consciousness is basically negative*.

I can recall sitting in a cinema as a child, and as the film ended suddenly realizing that I was feeling intensely happy and optimistic. I thought, 'Why am I feeling so happy?' and then remembered, 'Of course, we broke up from school today, and it's the beginning of the August holiday.' I was feeling happy, and yet the happiness had retreated into my subconscious mind. Not, please note, into the *unconscious* – only into that twilight realm between consciousness and the unconscious: the subconscious. You could compare these states of subconscious optimism to a kind of underfloor lighting which creates a kind of rosy glow and makes us feel happy and relaxed. The playwright Granville Barker called it: 'The secret life'. Healthy people have their underfloor lighting permanently switched on – which is why they find it so easy to have peak experiences. But consider again Graham Greene's experience of Russian roulette. When he pulled the trigger and there was just a click, 'It was if a light had been turned on and I saw that all life was infinitely beautiful.' He had switched on his underfloor lighting by deliberately inducing a crisis.

In the same way, I had an old friend who told me that his dog was subject to fits of depression. One day, he accidentally locked the dog in the cupboard and when it came out, it was bouncing with joy. From then on, whenever the dog became depressed, he would lock it in the cupboard for five minutes, and it would always emerge full of delight.

You see the absurdity? We feel bored or depressed, or just indifferent. A crisis presents itself and fills us with alarm. Then the crisis disappears, so the situation is basically the same as it was before the crisis presented itself. And yet we are now filled with a sense of delight. Moreover, this is not just a 'feeling'. We can *see*, now the crisis has vanished, that we have a thousand reasons for being glad to be alive. It is as if normal consciousness was somehow *blinkered*, like a blinkered horse. And crisis tears off the blinkers.

This is the absurd paradox of human existence. Man knows what he *doesn't* want far more clearly than he knows what he *does* want. As Fichte says: 'To *be* free is nothing; to *become* free is heaven.' There is something preposterous about this. It is like buying an expensive car, and discovering that it will do 90 miles an hour *in reverse* and only 10 miles an hour going forward. Nature seems to have made some kind of basic error in the human design.

Camus makes the same point in his novel *L'Étranger*. His hero Meursault, who has gone through the novel in a state of bored indifference, suddenly wakes up when he is on the point of death, about to be hanged for a murder he did not commit. As the priest tries to persuade him to repent, he suddenly loses his temper and shakes him until his teeth rattle. The result of this discharge of emotion is a sense of immense relaxation and happiness – a feeling of oneness with the universe. He makes the curious statement: 'I realized that I had been happy and I was happy still.' Is it possible to be happy and not to know it? Sperry discovered the answer to that question. It is perfectly possible for one side of the brain not to know what the other is feeling. But *real happiness*, such as Meursault experiences at the end of the novel, only happens when the left and right sides of the brain both feel the same thing.

The director of the BBC's music programme, Hans Keller, once described how, when he was in Germany in the 1930s and Jews were being put into concentration camps, he swore, 'If only I could get out of Germany alive I promise that I would never be unhappy for the rest of my life.' And, to a man whose life was in danger, it would seem obvious that it would be *so easy* to keep that promise. All he would have to do is to remember what it was like to expect to be arrested and thrown into a concentration camp.

In the same way, Raskolnikov, in *Crime and Punishment*, says, when he thinks he is going to be arrested and executed for murder, 'If I had to stand on a narrow ledge for ever and ever, in eternal darkness and eternal tempest, I would rather do that than die at once.' But what would he *do* on his narrow ledge? It is difficult to put into words, yet everyone of us can see the answer. Dr Johnson said that when a man is to be hanged in the morning, it concentrates his mind wonderfully.

When the mind is totally concentrated, full of a deep sense of purpose, the right and left brain suddenly begin to work in concert, and consciousness is transformed. Raskolnikov feels that he could stand on a narrow ledge for all eternity because he has the world inside his brain. He is like a man with the whole British Museum library inside his head. And we somehow know instinctively that this library is accessible to us when we can galvanize ourselves into a sense of urgency.

What we are now speaking about is what the Buddha meant by enlightenment. We have nearly translated this into Western terms. We are talking, in other words, about religion. Whenever we are able to relax and see life from a bird's-eye view, we recognize that we are happy and that life is intensely beautiful. This never fails to happen. Any crisis, any stimulus, will release that handbrake inside us, and enable us to go into deep relaxation and the peak experience.

Why then can we not do it except by dangerous expedients like Russian roulette or alcohol or drugs? The problem, we can see, lies in the underfloor lighting. When it is switched off, life is like a dull Sunday afternoon. Let me remind you again of Schumacher's words. 'We see not simply with our eyes but a great part of our mental equipment as well, and since this mental equipment varies greatly from person to person, there are inevitably many things that some people can see and others can't. In other words, for which some people are adequate and others not. When the level of the knower is not adequate to the level of the object of knowledge the result is not factual error but something much more serious: an inadequate and impoverished view of reality.' You could compare this impoverished view of reality to someone who went into a picture gallery lit only by dim lights, and who insists that he can see the pictures perfectly well. And so, in a sense, he can – in the sense of being able to describe any one of them. Yet if someone raised the blinds and let in the sunlight, he will suddenly recognize that he was *not* seeing the pictures. He was only half-seeing them.

And now, I think, we can begin to see our way towards the solution. At least, we have now started to define our terms fairly clearly. We know that everyday consciousness is narrow because it is restricted to left-brain awareness. It lacks that third dimension which is added by right-brain participation. Because we easily slip into boredom, our subconscious premises tend to be negative. We feel the world is basically rather a dull place. Sudden crisis has the effect of shaking the mind awake, and making us realise that the world is full of infinite potential. We were seeing the pictures with the blinds drawn.

If only we could clearly *recognize this*, if we could say it to ourselves again and again until we *know* it to be true, we could gradually reverse this negative assumption that underlies consciousness. *In short, what we must do is to reprogramme our underfloor lighting*.

In the 1890s, an American newspaper editor called Thomson J. Hudson became fascinated by hypnosis, and went on to write a classic book called *The Law of Psychic Phenomena*. His interest seems to have begun when he witnessed a hypnotic session in which a rather commonplace young man was placed in a trance by a professor of physiology. The young man was a Greek scholar and the professor pointed to an empty chair and said, 'Allow me to introduce you to Socrates.' The young man bowed reverently to the empty chair. The professor told him that he could ask Socrates any questions he liked – adding that, as Socrates was a spirit, the rest of them could not hear him. He asked the young man to repeat aloud what Socrates said. The young man proceeded to ask Socrates various questions, and then repeated his answers, which were so brilliant and apposite that some people present thought that perhaps the spirit of Socrates really was sitting in the chair. After Socrates, they introduced him to various other modern philosophers, and in each case the answers formed a brilliant and self-consistent system of philosophy.

What was happening, of course, is what happens when we dream that we are composing a piece of music, and actually hear magnificent music in our sleep. The right brain seems to have this capacity for sheer creativity.

Hudson observed many such cases, and concluded that we have two people living inside our heads – this was in 1893 – which he called the objective mind and the subjective mind. The objective mind looks out towards the external world and copes with everyday reality – in other words, the left brain. The subjective mind looks inward towards our inner being, and is in charge of our intuitions and our vital energy – in other words, the right brain. The subjective mind, said Hudson, is far more powerful than the objective mind. Under hypnosis, the objective mind is put to sleep, which explains why people become capable of far more under hypnosis than when they are awake. An old trick of stage hypnotists was to tell someone that he would become as stiff as a board, and that when he was placed between two chairs, with his head on one and his feet on the other, two men would jump up and down on his stomach without making him bend in the middle. And of course, he was able to do it. Yet it would have been totally impossible if he was awake. In other words, his 'subjective mind' – or right brain – could make him do extraordinary things *under the orders of the hypnotist*, and yet would not do them under the orders of his own left brain. Why not? Because the right brain believes the hypnotist, but it doesn't believe your left brain. If your left brain told it that it was going to lie between two chairs and support the weight of two men, it would sense the left brain's lack of confidence, and feel totally undermined.

The astonishing conclusion is that what is wrong with us is lack of 'left-brain confidence'. To our generation, this sounds an appalling heresy. D. H. Lawrence and Henry Miller have told us again and again that 'head consciousness' is dangerous and stupid and that we ought to trust the 'solar plexus' – by which they mean our instincts. That sounds very plausible, until we think about hypnosis. Then we can see that the problem is *not* that 'head consciousness' is overconfident and conceited, but that it is far too weak and diffident.

The translator, Richard Wilhelm, tells an interesting story that underlines the point. A remote Chinese village was suffering from drought, and they finally sent for a rain-maker from some distant province. When he arrived, he asked to be conducted to a house on the edge of the village and ordered them not to disturb him. For three days, no one heard or saw him. Then suddenly it began to rain heavily; in fact, it began to snow too. When the man emerged from the hut, Wilhelm asked him how he had succeeded in making rain. The rain-maker replied, 'I didn't make rain.' 'But it is raining', said Wilhelm. 'But I didn't make it rain', said the rain-maker. 'I come from a region where everything is in order. It rains when it should and is fine when that is needed. The people are also in order and in themselves. But that was not the case for the people here. They were all out of order and out of themselves. They were not living in the way of Tao. Their attitude infected me when I arrived, so I had to go away on my own for three days until I was once more in Tao. As soon as that happened, it rained naturally.'

In other words, the people of the village had become so infected with a sense of discouragement and defeat that they were somehow making things worse. As soon as they were 'in Tao' – that is, the right and left brains were working in harmony – Nature also fell into harmony, and it began to rain.

According to Taoism, our minds can somehow influence reality. In fact, they do influence reality all the time. If our minds are out of harmony, then so is reality. Jung seems to have had the same intuition when he recognized that 'synchronicity' is not merely another name for coincidence, but is something more meaningful. Synchronicity is a type of coincidence *caused by the mind*.

Maslow, as you know, died more than 20 years ago. Since then, I have come across one other thinker who seems to me to be of comparable importance. It is unlikely that you have heard his name. He is an American doctor called Howard Miller, and he wrote to me some time in the late 1970s. In his letters, he enclosed a couple of his papers. Like Thomson J. Hudson, Miller had become deeply interested in the mystery of hypnosis. One of his patients had been terrified of dental injections, and when he read in a newspaper an advertisement by a dentist that said he could draw teeth under hypnosis, Miller took his patient along to see him. The dentist placed her under hypnosis and then, to Miller's surprise, said, 'What is more, when I pull out the tooth you will not bleed.' This struck Miller as preposterous; you can't tell a person not to bleed. Yet indeed when the tooth came out the patient did not bleed.

Miller began to try it on his own patients. He discovered that he was good at hypnosis, and tried hypnotizing terminal cancer patients. He began to obtain astonishing remissions, which convinced him once again that there is something in the brain which is far more powerful than the ordinary conscious self.

However, Miller went a very important stage beyond Hudson. Miller asked himself, 'What is it that actually gives the order to the autonomic nervous system and prevents the bleeding?' His answer was, 'The hypnotist is *replacing* the "you" in your brain and giving the orders in its place. Which means that if the "you" in your brain could give the orders with sufficient authority, *you* could stop bleeding without the intervention of a hypnotist.'

(Incidentally, there is a hypnotist in the Wirral called Joe Keeton who *is* curing cancer patients by means of hypnosis – completely and totally curing them. He even had remarkable success with a girl whose heel had been completely destroyed in a motorcycle accident: he somehow caused her to regrow the heel under hypnosis. He believes that what he is doing is simply getting through deep into the autonomic nervous system and reactivating certain healing powers which all human beings possess.)

Now Miller said that the key to all this is the 'you', the person who lives in the cerebral hemispheres of the brain and which he calls 'the unit of pure thought'. (Miller holds the somewhat paradoxical view that the brain is a mere *amplifier* of thought, which somehow originates beyond the brain. This is why he calls the creator of thought 'the unit of pure thought'.)

I read all this, and thought, 'Very interesting, but it isn't new. All Miller has done is to rediscover what the philosopher Husserl called the "transcendental ego".' So I wrote back to Miller, thanking him for his papers and telling him about Husserl. He was obviously disappointed by my response.

About three months later, I had finished a very hard day's writing and I went out for a walk on the cliff. Now I have got used to the fact that if I have been writing hard and I go for a walk, I can't relax fully. My brain goes grinding on, and somehow I just don't enjoy the scenery. And I discovered a long time ago that the best way to induce a state of appreciation is to play a kind of 'Russian roulette' with myself. What I do is to tense myself as fully as I possibly can, and then when I am fully, totally tense, I let go. And when I do that, suddenly I can *see* the scenery, and I feel completely relaxed. Well, I did this on this particular occasion, and then found myself thinking, 'What precisely did you just do? What part of you gave the order?' And I answered, 'It was just *me* – my left brain.' Then I thought, 'No, surely, that is impossible. The left brain is just my logical self, and everyone knows that is the villain – the person who stands in the way of inspiration.' I brooded about it for the rest of my walk, and came to the conclusion that it *was* my left brain that had given the order. And my right had relaxed because the left gave it with sufficient determination and authority. Then, suddenly, I realized that Miller was completely and utterly right. I wrote to him that evening to tell him so. And I re-read his paper – *What is Thought?* – with far more attention.

What Miller points out is that the brain is basically an enormous computer. It was the surgeon Wilder Penfield who discovered that if, during brain surgery, he accidentally touched a point in the temporal cortex, the patient was suddenly flooded with detailed memories of his childhood. The experiment makes it very clear that our brain is an enormous library.

In the same way, when a tune gets stuck in your head, you feel as if your brain contains a gramophone record that has got stuck in the groove. We have, in other words, a feeling that we have no control over our own mental states.

Yet, said Miller, let us try a different experiment. Try closing your eyes and conjure up a mental image. You will quickly realize that you can, *on demand*, evoke from the brain any image you desire, and cause it to be projected on a kind of inner mental screen. Order your brain to produce an image of yourself on the beach, see yourself there in total reality, visualize the colour of your bathing suit, the feel of the sand, the heat of the sun . . . Now instantly *order* the scene to be changed; ask a new film to be brought out. Imagine yourself at the base of a very tall mountain, look up to its summit, feel the sting of the frosty air, hear the feet crunching on the icy snow – and now on command, dissolve the entire mountain. If you take the trouble, you can become aware of the distinction between your 'observer' and the scene you are observing. These scenes were being called into existence by the *thought* that preceded them. Your 'unit of pure thought' gave the order and your brain obeyed. You *are* in control of the computer.

What is wrong with human beings is basically that we do not *realize* that we are in control. 'Lack of this awareness', says Miller, 'has kept us from picking up the reins and taking control of our own brains.' The situation could be compared to a man sitting in the cinema, watching a film that seems completely scrambled and haphazard, and wondering what on earth has gone wrong in the projection room. He goes up into the projection room and discovers that, in fact, there is no one there. And then, with a sudden shock, he remembers: *he* himself is the projectionist. We can only take control of our brains, says Miller, when we recognize that we are the projectionists.

Now I would suggest that we have stumbled upon

two basic ideas that might form the foundation of a new religion. The first of these is the recognition that the 'you' is basically the master of consciousness: it is in charge of what goes on inside our heads. The second is that the way in which we can establish contact with the enormous powers of the 'hidden self' is by *reprogramming the subconscious mind* into a positive instead of a negative attitude. The Hindu saint Ramakrishna did it accidentally. He was in a state of misery and despair because his inner life had become dull and inert. In desperation, he seized a sword, and was about to drive it through his heart when he said, 'Suddenly, the Divine Mother revealed herself, and I was overwhelmed by waves of shining light.' The ecstasy was so intense that he became unconscious. He had experienced the state called *samadhi*. And from this time on, he only had to hear the name of the Divine Mother to go into *samadhi*. In other words, the experience had totally reprogrammed his subconscious mind, and he could induce *samadhi* by pushing a kind of mental button.

Now I think you should be able to see what I mean about reprogramming the subconscious. Whenever you experience any kind of delight, whenever you experience those momentary visions of intensity, it is important to hang on to them and use the insight to reprogramme your subconscious, because *this* is the best time to do it. Provided you do it in the moment of vision or insight, the subconscious can be totally reprogrammed. What you are trying to do is to *grasp* that 'bird's-eye vision' so that you can never forget it. It could be compared to trying to take a kind of aerial photograph, remembering all the salient points of the landscape below you before you plunge back to earth again.

One more example. When I was lecturing in Vancouver at Simon Frazer University, I spent a whole week talking to my students about these things, and at the end of that time I felt exhausted. I had been trying to teach them the 'pen trick' – the trick of driving yourself to a point of concentration where the brain almost rebels, and then deliberately forcing yourself one stage further. I told them about a friend of mine, Bill Powell, who used to climb Nelson's Column in Trafalgar Square. He used to do this by putting a huge belt around the Column and then edging his way up until his feet were level with the belt. He would then hitch the belt up, momentarily bending his knees and then walking up again until he was level with the belt. Bill said, 'The trouble is, when you are halfway up, your knees hurt like mad and you just want to relax. But, of course, if you do, you would go straight down to the bottom.' Well, it's the same with the discipline of the mind. And I told my students, 'When it hurts, for God's sake *don't* let go. You are nearly there.'

A couple of hours later, driving home to the motel where I was staying, I could look down on the whole of Vancouver and its bay. The lights were just coming on, and it looked beautiful. I found myself thinking, 'Isn't it absurd. It looks beautiful but I am too bloody tired to appreciate it.' And then suddenly I thought, 'Wilson, you fool, you have been telling them all day that when they are in this state, they are almost there.' I made a tremendous effort, and it happened instantly: the whole bay seemed to explode and become suddenly incredibly beautiful.

The absurd thing was that I had almost forgotten. I was allowing my brain to churn on mechanically, merely looking forward to getting back home and pouring myself a drink. This is the danger: giving way to our *automatic mechanisms*. Yet because I knew, intellectually, that I could do it, I was able to side-step the mechanisms and achieve the peak experience. And I did it basically by suddenly *remembering* to make the additional effort.

We *can* do it. The power is already there in the brain. Everything is already there inside us. The Buddha was right: the key to peace lies inside us and always has. And now we can begin to understand it in Western scientific terms, it means that 'enlightenment' is no longer one of those mystical words with no precise meaning.

One final thought. Maslow discovered that when he began to talk to his students about peak experiences, they began to remember all kinds of occasions on which they'd had peak experiences – occasions that they'd almost forgotten about. And as soon as they began to remember and discuss peak experiences, *they began having peak experiences all the time*. Merely talking and thinking about it had reprogrammed the subconscious.

Most Western thinkers seem to agree that the world is in an appalling state, and that the correct attitude is pessimism tempered by cautious hope. For my own part, I believe that man has arrived at the most interesting point in his evolution, and that the future has never looked more promising. It is because Schumacher shared that sense of optimism that I hold his memory in so much affection.

V

Industrialism and American Indian Culture

Russell Means

Now I suppose that, by focusing on capitalism and Marxism as opposite sides of the same coin, which is European culture, and then contrasting that coin to a completely different one, which is American Indian culture, I'm opening myself up to charges of being 'simplistic'. It can and probably will be argued that I've left too many points uncovered.

Let me say that this seems like an intentional and petty diversion of attention from the real issues to be considered; *nobody* can address all the particular points open to discussion in a subject area as vast as comparing cultures, especially not in the context of a single essay or speech. The object is to break out positions clearly, illustrate them enough to get the point across, and then trust in your audience to be able to think their respective ways through all the possible variations which are appropriate to their situations. So I'll grant the 'critics' their point here; they're entirely welcome to it since it's totally irrelevant anyway.

Meanwhile, allow me to take a couple of other tendencies of so-called 'opposition to the status quo': trends which are not necessarily Marxist in their direct orientation, but which – as we shall see – follow a similar course of reinforcing the European order in the end. These I term as the 'arrogance of human rights' and the 'ignorance of civil rights'. They may be considered in order, and then certain of *their* sub-parts or variations may be dealt with. I do this to illustrate that the same rules apply to other tendencies within the European tradition that apply to the main points such as Christianity, capitalism and Marxism.

The notion of human rights has been rhetorically employed by virtually all sides of the European political and philosophical equations in recent years. As is well known, the Carter administration used this device in attempting to separate itself in the public mind from the brutal legacy of Nixonian Republican policies which had led to overt genocide in South-East Asia, a linkage which is partially true but which obviously ignores the roles of the Kennedy and Johnson 'liberal democrat' administrations in massively establishing US savagery there.

Those opposed to Carter's smokescreen, covering 'business as usual' by US power, attacked his administration on the basis that his 'human rights' concerns were directed primarily at Marxist countries. The treatment of Soviet Jews and the policies of the Pol Pot regime in Kampuchea are two prominent examples. Meanwhile, Carter's administration was actively supporting governments such as that of the Shah of Iran, Suharto's Indonesian government (which is busily exterminating East Timorese), Stroessner's regime in Paraguay (which is exterminating Ache Indians), the Chilean Junta of August Pinochet, Samoza's private empire in Nicaragua, the Pretoria apartheid regime in Azania (South Africa), Ian Smith's in Zimbabwe (Rhodesia), the Brazilian state which is conducting outright extermination of the Amazon Basin tribes. . . . The list could go on and on.

The more perceptive opponents to Carter's so-called human rights policies also pointed to the fact that his administration was conducting similar deprivations of rights against people *inside* the United States itself;

American Indians, the original occupants of this country, of course, are the classic victims of such abuse. So, said the critics, Carter was rather hypocritically condemning his ideological enemies for policies he himself was quite guilty of duplicating. And again, many of these critics and opponents of Carter were not ideological Marxists.

First, I agree that every conceivable right of individual human beings has been and is being violated globally by the Soviet Union and other Marxist states. I guess that's a point for Carter and Reagan, if you want to look at things that way. Second, I agree that Carter and Reagan are violating exactly the same rights, and they have done so on an even grander scale, which is a point for the other side. This is exactly what I've been saying throughout this talk: that it's six of one and half a dozen of the other. Marxism and capitalism are just flip sides of the coin of European cultural tradition: ultimately, they mean and they do the same thing.

This all goes directly to the notion of 'human rights' itself. This is a crystalline example of the insistence of the European tradition in elevating humans above and beyond the natural order, as beings with a unique privilege above the natural world. The assumption of these so-called rights constitutes a gross arrogance, a wilful disruption of natural balance and harmony by Euro-thinkers. It is human chauvinism, for lack of a better term.

Now, I don't want to be misinterpreted on this point. When I reject this arrogance of human rights, it does not mean that I reject the rights of oppressed people to freedom from the sorts of abuse they are currently suffering at the hands of Marxism and capitalism. To the contrary, I affirm their right to such freedom with every fibre of my being. But I do so not in the sense that they are somehow *uniquely* entitled *as human beings* to freedom from wanton exploitation and destruction. No, I insist on their rights as *natural* beings; I insist that they enjoy the same freedom from violation that is the right of a mountain to be free of strip mining, a field from being covered with asphalt, a river from being dammed or polluted. I reject the idea that one people have a right to trample or exterminate another in the same sense that I reject the idea that humans had or have the right to destroy the buffalo, the carrier pigeon, the caribou, or any of our relatives.

I don't know how to make this any clearer: human rights simply do not and cannot exist other than in the context of natural rights, the natural order. And within the natural order, the place of human beings is a minor ingredient. Those who delude themselves to the contrary, who insist upon violating nature by insisting on an artificial importance for humans within the natural order, accomplish only the opposite. They inevitably destroy their habitat, and thereby the basis for human life itself. *Only* when the natural rights of *all* relations are respected and inviolate can there be human rights, not as something special or superior, but as an integral part of the sacred hoop of life. In any other sense, there are no human rights at all. By this I mean that the natural order shall *withdraw* the privilege currently granted to the human species to exist. A continued arrogance by humans in this regard shall be repaid in full; that much is clear to anyone able to throw off the blinders of Euro-thinking long enough to look around themselves.

But I also spoke of something I termed 'the ignorance of civil rights'. In other words, civil rights are the special interests claimed by the members of a group on the basis of membership alone and at the direct expense of members of other groups.

For all that is obviously wrong with the idea of human rights, it is still a vastly superior concept to civil rights. The latter really comes down to base *greed*, the sharing of a stolen pie with the original thieves. Let's examine this in relation to the United States.

During the late 1950s and early 1960s, the Black population of the United States undertook what has come to be known as the 'Civil Rights Movement'. Within this movement, certain demands were formulated: the right to vote was asserted, the right to buy houses in any given neighbourhood was sought, the right to be educated was pushed, the rights to be employed at decent paying jobs, to eat in the same restaurants and to drink at the same drinking fountains as Whites were demanded. Again, the list could go on and on.

There was (and is) a certain validity to such demands. Black people were *not* equal to Whites in these areas. And in most cases they still aren't. But if you measure gains over the past twenty years against the demands of the Civil Rights Movement during the early '60s, you'll find that Blacks have garnered significant victories. Blacks are, relatively speaking, *much* less discriminated against at the polls than they were in 1960. In fact, the so-called Black Voters' Block has become an acknowledged force in American electoral politics. There are, *per capita*, vastly more Black college graduates now than there were in 1960 (including a substantial number of Ph.D.s, etc.). In a relative sense, substantial numbers of jobs have opened up which have, in turn, provided the ways and means for a lot of Blacks to move into the suburbs or wherever it was that housing discrimination seemed most rampant.

All this doesn't mean, of course, that ghettos have disappeared, that Blacks are now holding real power by being elected President or promoted to the boards of major corporations and banks. But it does mean that certain concrete wins have been had relative to the issues and formulated goals of the early '60s. This is at least true enough to have lent substance to White fears of socio-economic displacement, a virulent backlash including a new prominence for the Ku Klux Klan, and so on. It is at least theoretically possible to state that by following the course of action espoused, through the Civil Rights Movement for a long enough period of time, Black people would experience *full* wins in every area addressed by that movement. But what would this mean in practical terms?

It seems reasonable to draw up the following scenario: both ghettos and rural poverty would eventually be eliminated for Blacks because they were going to college and graduating, and being educated to hold important jobs in major corporations, a number of which would be headed by Black men and women; this would provide the economic basis for virtually all Blacks to live wherever they wished in America. It would also provide the basis for Blacks not only to eat in any restaurant they selected, but to own many of them. And then there's the question of electoral politics: the same economic base would provide for the massive support of Black candidates to offices up to and including that of President of the United States. As I said, it's at least theoretically possible to conjure up this image of the satiation of all major civil rights demands. Blacks *might* achieve an 'equal split of the American pie', but at what cost?

Well, consider a Black president of the Chase Manhattan Bank, for example. He or she would, through the success of a long and rather bloody civil rights struggle, at last be head of a gigantic financial institution foundationed on the international exploitation of peoples (not to mention environments, for the moment) in places like South Africa, Namibia, Zimbabwe, Zaire, Mozambique, Brazil, Argentina, Chile, Paraguay, Venezuela, Malaysia, Thailand, Navajo, the Black Hills; there's no need to go on with the list. And there's no way that this Black woman or man could alter the situation to any significant degree, since this is the basis of his or her business. Without this international exploitation – called 'profit' by bankers – the Chase Manhattan business empire would immediately collapse, thus instantly ending the position gained for Blacks within it through decades of struggle.

Clearly, this is an absurd goal for a movement allegedly intended to better the lot of non-European peoples. And it doesn't matter which corporation you pick to make as an example: General Motors or Exxon or US Steel or Anaconda Copper or Bell Aircraft or the Adolph Coors Corporation or Aetna Finance – the same principle holds in each case. This is also true of attaining political power in America: the primary mission of the President of the United States is, after all, to keep the gears of American business meshing, both at home and abroad.

Every posh suburban residence occupied by a Black, every executive salary line, every single 'gain' achieved through the logic of civil rights comes out of the blood, sweat and tears of other *non*-European peoples. If you wish to look at things in terms of human rights, every gain in civil rights terms for Black people in the US can *only* accrue by displacing the cost onto other non-Europeans elsewhere. And beyond the arrogance of assessing the costs merely in terms of human consequences, the entire environment, our habitat, must pay the price of civil rights 'equality'.

To gain equality with the European on his own terms, one must become just *like* him; must think, talk, act and destroy like him. On a truly massive scale, this is the process of identifying with and emulating the oppressor, which psychiatrists have pointed out lately in individual cases, as being the extremely irrational behaviour of a hostage in relation to his or her captor. This is the logic and behaviour of accepting that Europe's global imperialism is not only acceptable but correct, that European supremacy is real, that *non*-European 'success' means becoming the mirror image of Europe. This is what I mean when I speak of the *ignorance* of civil rights, because I believe that ultimately very few Black people really wish to participate in such a process and 'achieve' such results.

In fact, I'd wager that nobody would own up to seeking truly to live in luxury in America at the direct expense either of their Black sisters and brothers in southern Africa or of my Lakota People on Pine Ridge. You can say to me that the Civil Rights Movement I refer to is ancient history, that your goals and aspirations have changed dramatically since the days of the Mississippi Freedom Rides. Up to a point, I have to agree with you. This objection is absolutely true and correct, as far as it goes. But let me ask you a question: Is there anyone here who *strenuously* objects to my constantly referring to *Blacks*?

What is a Black? Or in the case of human beings, to what does Black refer? Genetic structure, pure and simple. Black skin or white skin or yellow, brown or red skin is merely a genetic condition. It determines *only* how a person looks, not how he or she acts, thinks, feels, etc. And yet in America the offshoots of the Civil Rights Movement have been Black Power, Black Pride and Black Awareness. Even here, there seems to be a general acceptance that Black is *the* distinctive characteristic of pride and strength. I'd like to examine this assumption for a moment.

It seems to me that the term 'Black' gained popular currency in this country during a period roughly from 1963–65. At the time it constituted a conscious rejection of a Euro-imposed term, 'negro' – a thoroughly derogatory and colonial term – and the imposition of another, much more prideful term that was selected by the people thus labelled. To this I say: right on! This was a process of taking one of European racism's best shots and turning it on its head: a decolonizing act, a revolutionary act if you prefer. This represented, at the time, a major psychological breakthrough among the second-largest single *non*-European population in North America.

I know that in and of itself, the whole notion of race pride ultimately leads nowhere. It demolishes the ability to make distinctions, allies and positive gains. This is one reason, which I repeat over and over, why I look to culture rather than race as being really important. I've experienced and I sympathize with the moment of race pride, but once it's over, I say let's get on with content, with thinking, feeling and acting, with respect for *all* of life.

In the case at hand, I reject the long-term utility of the concept of 'Blackness' as emphatically as I reject the notions of White, Red, Yellow or Brown as explanatory of anything other than pigmentation and perhaps bone structure. Black is, in the long run, no more nor less than the genetic division of the American imperial pie, a negative force in the universe, a term based entirely in the civil rights context of demanding that the American power structure allow non-Whites to *join* it. The people I am interested in meeting, in reaching and in allying with are *Africans*. There is not a Black in America who does not have his or her real cultural roots in Africa. You are Africans in the same sense that I am American Indian or that Ronald

Reagan is a European. Beyond that, you are specifically Bantu or Watusi or Zulu or Masai in precisely the same sense that I am Lakota or that Ronald Reagan is a German (whether he knows it or not). Like I said, it's time to get beyond that moment of self-recognition and on into real content and substance. Who we are is much, much more than our DNA structure. We are each the product of thousands of generations of cultural continuity, wisdom and tradition. If you are not wholeheartedly engaged in linking yourself to the heritage of Africa which is rightfully yours, then the chances are you are linking yourself directly to the heritage of Europe, the heritage of the oppressor. This linkage of black-skinned people to the European tradition is what I consider to be the greatest danger of the ignorance of civil rights – a danger which *must* be overcome, and quickly.

Again, I don't want to be misunderstood here. I'm not attempting to reinvent Marcus Garvey's 'back-to-Africa movement'. And I'm not an anthropologist attempting to define the African cultural heritage in terms of overt physical expression. What I'm talking about are the essential cultural ingredients which make up values, world-view and spiritual tradition. I believe that African culture, in the latter sense, is perfectly appropriate and completely viable right here and right now. I say this in precisely the same sense that I insist that American Indian culture and tradition is necessary, not some idiot's conception of Hiawatha but *the* valid alternative to the European order in the Americas.

Africans are tribal peoples, natural peoples. Despite hundreds of years of European exploitation and genocide, they have never given up that value structure, that world view, their sense of spiritual integration into the natural order. Europeans, on the other hand, *were* tribal peoples but, with a few exceptions – and remember, exceptions only prove the rule – gave that up and demand now that the rest of the planet follow their lead into an artificial universe.

Because of the historical conditions surrounding the African transplantation into this hemisphere, it has been impossible for people of African descent in this country to maintain cultural continuity in the same fashion as have American Indians. This does not, however, prevent the energy of African Americans from going into the reconstitution of their true cultural heritage. To the extent that *you* seek to realize *your* heritage, you are the natural allies of American Indians and all other natural beings. You are welcome here and considered as partners in the struggle for natural rights.

For those who think it can't be done, or that even the *form* of struggle is pointless, I suggest you look southward to Surinam. Right now, there is a village, established generations ago by runaway slaves. The originators of this village were representative of a number of African tribal cultures. What these people did, and what their descendants *continue* to do, is to act upon their common characteristics of values and their oldest world-view (this is shared by *all* natural cultures). This strength allowed them to overcome their superficial differences and thereby establish a true community of *resistance* which has stood the test of time: *a self-sufficient* community of Africans in this hemisphere, following aeons of respect for the natural order, proves it can be done. And remember, my relatives, the Red People welcomed and made room for them . . . I want each and every one of you to consider, acknowledge and remember that the African slaves' first taste of freedom in this hemisphere was provided by American Indian peoples.

To the extent that you forgo your heritage in favour of identifying with Europe, with the sanctity of purely human rights and, worse, civil rights, you are as unwelcome as the European. I don't worry that you might be unnecessarily insulted or 'alienated' by such a statement; only those who would seek to equivocate on unequivocal matters will see fit to be offended by such a position. Those who view themselves as beyond 'the pale' of Europe and all that it has come to stand for have never objected to clarification of the issues in such a matter. It is these people who are my allies and with whom I seek to communicate; as relations of the natural order, we have much in common and much to discuss.

The others, as Frantz Fanon so aptly put in, are but 'black skins/white masks'. They are invited to join the Marxists, the anarchists, Peter McDonald's Vichy Indians and other functionaries of the many faces of Euro-culture in history's gallery of sell-outs, rip-offs and oppressors.

To some it may seem that I am singling out the African experience in America since 1960 as exclusively representative of certain errors. I have no wish to scapegoat a group in this fashion, and have no intention of allowing matters to rest there. Civil rights preoccupations are not the peculiar domain of African activists. However, it must be said that Africans constituted the cutting edge, the vanguard of contemporary civil rights struggles, and are therefore the logical initial focus when one begins to discuss the issue of civil rights.

I might further add that I'm not saying that civil rights was not a reasonable place for Africans to begin their struggle. Given the general consciousness of the early 1960s, produced in large part by historical discontinuities generated by slavery and other forms of European genocide, civil rights struggles may well have been the *only* place to begin. And for having begun, under the conditions of the time, all Africans have reason to be proud.

The question in this connection is one of getting beyond the beginnings of a struggle, of increasing the level of consciousness beyond the initial moment of awareness and pride. It seems to me that it is entirely possible to create African Awareness out of Black Pride, to recreate Africans from Blacks, to proceed from civil rights to human rights to natural rights in one continuous cycle. So I don't dismiss the historical importance of the Civil Rights Movement, the people involved, or the motives behind the struggles of the early 1960s. I simply reject that it was ever a valid end in itself, or that it holds a continuing relevance today. It is not the pioneers of the Civil Rights Movement who strike me as a negative force; it's those hangers-on who build lucrative careers on the bones of that movement right now, today. In any event, it is now 1980, not 1960.

And, of course, there are also extra-legal forms of discrimination such as rape (currently up nearly 40 per cent from 1975), mutilation, beatings, sexual harrass-ment of the non-forcible variety, and murder. All of this is so blatantly prevalent within the social main-stream that it seems unquestionable that it is integral to the structure of the United States. There is absol-utely no way that any right-thinking person can observe the situation and not conclude that these are critical issues, not only for the people most directly affected but for *all* relations.

But consider the general 'solutions' to these prob-lems as proposed and fought for by the activists of each group. Various tactics are employed to ensure that gays and women gain equal access to employment and pro-motional opportunities, credit opportunities, access to housing, and general legal status. Who is the equality that is being sought measured against? White men. Or, to be more specific, White Anglo-Saxon Protestant heterosexual men: the infamous 'norm' of the European mainstream. Once again, when confronted with the oppressor, entire groups* opt not to eliminate him but to become like him, not to dismantle the industrial society of values and outlooks which oppress them but to join it, to *demand* to participate in it.

It's rather easy to see where such demands lead. Every short-term gain garnered by women and gays in the civil rights context represents a slightly longer-term loss for another oppressed group. Consider so-called 'Affirmative Action' legislation sought by the League of Women Voters, the National Organization of women and other primary women's civil rights lobbies. Under the guidelines which resulted from this act, both women and 'minorities' come under what are called 'protected classes'. Hence, they are perpetually competing, one against the other, for the same positions.

I don't know of any clearer example of divide and conquer tactics: two groups which are oppressed by the same third group are duped into constantly competing against each other rather than joining forces as natural allies to end their mutual oppression. And what does either group get if it happens to be 'the winner' of a job on a given day? Well, current mythology holds that every job which goes to women or minorities undercuts the ultimate power of WASP males; altogether then, enough jobs awarded under Affirmative Action would

---

* As an aside, at this point, I'd like to note that I don't intend to generalize an entire sex of any culture as following only one course. My remarks are geared to the women's movement in its primary form. There are always exceptions which serve to prove the rule. If you are the exception, you will not be offended by what I say. But if the shoe fits, wear it.

serve to topple the power structure of this country. I submit that this is purely absurd. Jobs have functions within the structure. Therefore, every time a woman, a gay person, or a non-European accepts a position within the structure, they become functional *parts* of it. Rather than raising opposition to the status quo, Affirmative Action serves to reinforce the industrial society substantially.

It's appropriate to point out that, rather than reinforcing the power of their oppressors, it would be more reasonable for women and gays to seek out natural allies. Clearly the planet has traditions and alternatives to offer beyond the narrow confines of the European status quo. I will use as examples of this aspect those with which I am most familiar: the traditions of my own Lakota culture.

Consider first the situation of gays, as it seems the least complex issue. In European culture, homosexuals are discriminated against precisely because they are socially aberrant. This, in biblical terms, is considered 'abnormal' and is a crime against the Judaeo-Christian god. Thus, homosexuality is irrevocably condemned as bad within the European tradition.

Now, homosexuality existed and exists within Lakota culture, as it does in any society. But our way of viewing it was and is rather different from the European practice. Understand that this is an aberration within Lakota society in precisely the same sense as in Europe. But for exactly that reason, because homosexuality is not the norm within Lakota culture, my people have always looked to these individuals as special, as selected within the natural order as chosen to bear a different vision and add a certain balance to life.

I think you can see where this leads: in their scramble for civil rights, gays manage only to reinforce a cultural context which rejects them out of hand against cultures

111

which have traditionally accorded them every respect as natural relations. If this makes sense, it can only be in terms of the logic of self-defeat.

Concerning women, as I said, this is a much more complex issue, I've already addressed the status of women within European culture, so now I'd like to speak of their role within Lakota culture. To do so, I'd like to begin with a story told to me by my grandfather when I was a young boy:

A long time ago, at the beginning, some Lakotas were sitting around a fire. As they sat there, the men in the group noticed the women growing with child. As they watched, they witnessed the miracle of birth. And as they continued to watch, they saw the women nurturing life at their breasts. After a time, the men began to discuss among themselves what they had seen. Much talk occurred and then the men concluded, and rightfully, that they stood for very little in the cycle of life.

After a time of wondering what they were good for, the men grew envious of the women. From there on, they began to pout and play games as a means to draw attention to an importance they could only pretend to possess.

The point of this story is that it was told to me as it is told, in one variation or another, to all Lakota males at a young age. Lakota men begin to learn very early that women are a source of life and nurturing strength of a sort which is denied to men. A traditional Lakota man grows up and goes through his entire life acting in accordance with this basic knowledge. It is wisdom central to the entire Lakota lifeway.

All of this is not empty rhetoric or gloss. It is the substance of much of day-to-day Lakota life. Let's consider some of the implications. Take, for example, the concept of a Lakota warrior. First, let me state categorically that the notion that warrior status is, was or ever will be restricted exclusively to men is false. There have been women warriors throughout the history of the Lakota people, there are women warriors today and you may rest assured there will be in the future. But they are the exceptions, the aberrations if you will, who prove the rule. They are special people to the Lakota.

In any event, the rule that I was referring to is *not* that warriors should be men (which is a European rule), but that a Lakota should treat all relations with respect. Now war is a dangerous occupation; people tend to die in wars. Lakota men recognized early on that in assuming the warrior's responsibility for defence of the people they could acknowledge a certain respect for women, for women's ability to give and nurture life. The respect occurs in the process of acknowledging the women's power by relieving them of the dangerous but relatively minor responsibility of fighting. In a real sense, Lakota men announce ultimate respect to Lakota women because we are naturally more expendable than the women.

Let's return momentarily to the existence of warrior women, because it proves two things which have to do with the respectful relations I'm speaking of. First, it demonstrates that Lakota women could and can, when there's a real need, handle the warrior's chores. Thus, it can be seen that Lakota women have *allowed* men to assure this social role.

Second, Lakota women tend to allow their men the warrior's role out of respect for the men's feelings. After all, this does provide the men with a certain social value which would otherwise be lacking. And true to form, Lakota men have traditionally developed the serious business of community defence into a game.

For the most part, that's what war was among American Indian peoples before European soldiers came with their ideas of extermination and body counts . . . a game. It took the absurdity of being faced with outright genocide to force American Indians to become serious killers in self-defence.

But pre-contact warfare was one of the major games through which Lakota women allowed Lakota men to draw attention to their accomplishments and cultural value. Clearly, we are not talking of a system of discrimination and imbalance; we are speaking of a balanced system of respect between the sexes and the future generations. We are speaking in terms of a fundamental harmony with the natural order.

All this leads into other functional aspects of daily Lakota life. For example, the nature of the roles adopted by Lakota men determined that their lifespans were apt to be considerably shorter than those of the women. Thus, it is natural that the women were looked to as the formal lineage of social continuity. Men went to live in the villages of their wives; ancestry was determined through the mother. Contrast this to European culture where men also live for shorter periods than women, but a paternal structure is nonetheless enforced in violation of all natural reason. To a certain extent, the colonial process undertaken by Europe has imposed a paternal veneer upon Lakota culture, but this is a skin easily shed through decolonization. Under conditions of real lifespans, a maternal structure is merely acknowledgement of and respect for the obvious.

The natural strength of women has obvious effects within Lakota life beyond the transmission of cultural continuity. The obvious nurturing capacity of women, which is lacking in men, leads directly to social roles of nurturing for women; they feed the people. Men

114

provide what is fed, but this is an act of compensation, a means of achieving balance and harmony once again. There's no question that Lakota women can, when need be, also provide the food which is eaten; they allow men this role to assist in creating balance and harmony. Once again, this is a matter of mutual respect between the sexes and between the Lakota and the natural order.

Women are the strength, the pride and the continuation of the Lakota culture and the Lakota people. Compared to the women, Lakota men remain children all their lives. Try as they may, they can never catch up with the power that women possess naturally. Ask any old Lakota woman. She can tell you that the older men become, the more they become aware of the unevenness of the race and the more childlike they seem.

Perhaps the clearest example of the complete reversal of the status accorded women within the Lakota tradition as compared to that of Europe has to do with what theology professors like to call 'deities'. You are aware, no doubt, that within Christian doctrine, God is assumed to be male. The Christian God is referred to as 'he'; 'man' is made in the Christian God's image; 'his' son (also the 'father's' splitting image) came to Earth as the Messiah, Jesus Christ, and was a strangely WASPish looking character from the alleged representations I've seen. In effect, European males selected what they fancied as the mirror image of themselves to serve as their god, not realizing that 'image' meant the goodness of the great mystery – e.g. respect, patience, humility, virtue, responsibility and wisdom.

Lakota people, on the other hand, see themselves as having originated through a woman, the White Buffalo Calf Woman. Two things are striking about this. First, this so-called deity is female, which acknowledges the natural *fact* that all people originate through the fe-

115

male. Second, this female is not like any woman you'll ever meet. She is, as a buffalo woman, totally integrated into her other relations. This twin rejection, that of male supremacy and that of human supremacy, are the twin cornerstones upon which the Lakota spiritual tradition, the entire Lakota culture, is built.

It should come as no surprise to anyone that today's Christians and their capitalist and Marxist decendants, feeling that they have established dominion over the Earth and all relations associated with it, are now busily destroying the whole world in their asinine assumption that 'progress and development' are godlike, and therefore limitless. If you think this is pushing the point too far, look around you at the spread of industrial 'progress'. Who else but self-appointed gods could take it upon themselves to create vehicles of species suicide and then define them as good?

In the old days, the troops and the commissioners would come from Washington and demand that the 'headman' of the Lakota meet with them. When people who were wiser than they attempted to explain that no Lakota, least of all a man, had the power over other Lakotas they were seeking, they still insisted. They were adamant because this was how they understood social power based on their heritage as Europeans. The very notion of male supremacy was imported to this hemisphere from Europe . . . along with whisky, smallpox, scalping and venereal disease.

Now, I realize that the women's movement is not necessarily Marxist in its outlook. It is, after all, an avowed civil rights movement rather than an avowed revolutionary one. But I submit to you, that the women's movement proceeds from precisely the same assumptions, when it comes to non-European culture, as does Marxism. Or capitalism and Christianity, for that matter. This means that they proceed from a very

116

limited context which they understand – European culture – and then rather arrogantly assert that their understanding applies universally.

I'm not saying the problems these European women experience in their own lives aren't real. They are, and I've already mentioned a few of them. But the problems are peculiarities of the nature of European culture, not something universally inherent to men and women. In a sense, you can't blame them, never having benefited from living in a context of mutual respect, for the error. This, however, fails to diminish the supreme arrogance and ignorance they exhibit when they impose their analysis outside their own arena.

Consider the following, all of which have been laid on me by one or another European feminist during the past few years. One woman observed to me that the predominantly male membership of the Lakota warrior societies was evidence of our 'sexism'. In European society, of course, this would be true but, as we have seen, the exact opposite is true among the Lakota. Another presented me with the profound insight that Lakota society was and is a 'patriarchy' because 'all the chiefs have been men'. All the chiefs, in the sense that Europeans understand the term, were the invention of Europe. In the true Lakota sense of social power, as we have also seen, women have always held a balance.

Once again, the author of this feminist analysis would probably have been on very firm ground had she been examining a situation originating in European culture. In that culture, menstruation is perceived as filthy, disgusting, as something to be hidden and avoided both in fact and in polite conversation. The monthly cycle is even referred to, in quasi-religious terms, as 'women's curse'. But in Lakota culture, things are very different.

To a Lakota, the fact of women's menstruation is

considered as a blessing. It is a natural process through which the women are cleansed by the great mystery, a power obviously denied to men. One result of this may, by now, be predictable. Lakota men are engaged throughout their lives in actions designed to balance the situation, to compensate through effort for that which the women possess naturally and without effort. For example, one of our major so-called 'religious rights' is the sweat lodge, a purifying place, a place of honour and cleansing. Lakota men *must* regularize their participation in the sweats as a means to balance the natural cleansing of the women's natural monthly cycle. And within the sweat, we pray our thanks to the universe for that same monthly cleansing of our women. Other aspects of our ceremonial life, including the Sun Dance, carry the same sort of implications. Of course, in the process of offering up her 'penetrating analysis of Lakota sexism', the feminist author was no doubt totally unaware of all this.

No doubt, then, she would have been most surprised to discover what could have been readily accessible information, had she bothered to consult with a traditional Lakota woman, rather than arrogantly assuming she was already aware of the answers *before* beginning her 'study'.

As the Christian would 'save our souls' by converting us to a suicidal world-view, as capitalist and Marxist alike would solve our 'primitive' economic status by industrializing us and thereby destroying our habitat, so too would feminism 'solve' the 'problem' of our 'sexism' by destroying the fundamental respect between men and women which is a core aspect of our culture. It should be clear to anyone who cares to consider it that each of these European tendencies amounts to genocide: no more, no less.

This brings me to another dual point. First, while

I've utilized the Lakota culture as my illustration for the points I've covered concerning women and gays, the person who considers things with open eyes will perceive that what I've said is clearly relevant to the roles and status of women and gays in all natural societies. There are, of course, vast ranges of variation in the specific social practices involved on a culture-by-culture basis, but the reality here is that I've been speaking of natural relations, and you may rest assured that any natural culture or society will, by definition, conform to the order of these relations in its own fashion. And I don't care whether you are considering Bantu culture in Africa, h'Mong culture in the Laotian highlands, Moro culture in the Philipines, Ache culture in the southern part of this hemisphere, or the Inuit in the far north; you will find the natural order prevailing.

The second part of this point is that women of colour are *not* ignorant of such facts. This accounts for the extremely low participation of women of colour within the women's movement over the years. Women of colour have understood all along that their men were not their enemy. They *know* who their enemies really are.

And this isn't to say that sexism, real sexism, doesn't exist within contemporary non-European societies, the Lakota included. I've never said that it doesn't. What I've said is that it doesn't exist within Lakota *culture*. What this means is that many non-European societies, including the Lakota, have been colonized for generations by Europe. One of the costs absorbed by a colonized people is that certain of its members become 'acculturated' and begin to assimilate into the society of the oppressor; this is an integral part of the process of European genocide. Those members of the colonized people who become assimilated take on the values, the world-view and thus the behavioural characteristics of the colonizing culture; for myself, I call these people 'Vichy Indians', who sell out their people to would-be conquerors.

As this pertains to sexism in Lakota and other non-European societies today, it means that the men who are guilty of such conduct are adopting the mannerisms of Europe. To the extent that they are sexist, they are Vichy, they are European, *not* Lakota in any meaningful sense. Our women understand this, and this understanding leads them to the wisdom that the conflict is between cultures, not between sexes. The solution to the problem, such as it exists, of sexism in contemporary Lakota society is the full-fledged assertion of the Lakota culture, not its abandonment. And the same holds true for all the natural peoples of the world.

I've talked about a number of different problems so far. The fact which cannot be escaped, no matter how you twist it, is that they all have the same source: the industrial society and culture of Europe. Industrialism *cannot* exist without exploiting and degrading the earth. This is not debatable: it is a *fact*. In exploiting and degrading the earth, industrialism *necessarily* exploits and degrades every single creature which lives upon or within it. And this obviously includes human beings. Look around you. . . .

VI

People, Land and Community

Wendell Berry

To presume to describe land, work, people and community by information, by quantities, seems invariably to throw them into competition with one another. Work is understood to exploit the land, the people to exploit their work, the community to exploit its people. And then instead of land, work, people, and community, we have the industrial categories of resources, labour, management, consumers and government. We have exchanged harmony for an interminable fuss, and the work of culture for the timed and harried labour of an industrial economy.

I would like to speak more precisely than I have before of the connections that join people, land and community – to describe, for example, the best human use of a problematical hillside farm. In a healthy culture these connections are complex. The industrial economy breaks them down by oversimplifying them, and in the process raises obstacles that make it hard for us to see what the connections are or ought to be. These are mental obstacles, of course, and there appear to be two major ones:

The assumption that knowledge (information) can be 'sufficient'.

The assumption that time and work are short.

These assumptions will be found implicit in a whole set of contemporary beliefs: that the future can be studied and planned for; that limited supplies can be wasted without harm; that good intentions can safeguard the use of nuclear power. A recent American newspaper article says, for example, that 'A congressionally mandated study of the Ogallala Aquifier is finding no great cause for alarm from [sic] its rapidly dropping levels. The director of the . . . study . . says that even at current rates of pumping, the aquifier can supply the Plains with water for another 40 or 50 years . . . All six states participating in the study . . . are forecasting increased farm yields based on improved technology.' Another article speaks of a different technology with the same optimism: 'The nation has invested hundreds of billions of dollars in atomic weapons and at the same time has developed the most sophisticated strategies to fine-tune their use to avoid a holocaust. Yet the system that is meant to activate them is the weakest link in the chain . . . Thus, some have suggested that what may be needed are warning systems for the warning systems.'

Always the assumption is that we can first set demons at large, and then, somehow, become smart enough to control them. This is not childishness. It is not even 'human weakness'. It is a kind of idiocy, but perhaps we will not cope with it and save ourselves until we regain the sense to call it evil.

The trouble, as in our conscious moments we all know, is that we are terrifyingly ignorant. The most learned of us are ignorant. The acquisition of knowledge always involves the revelation of ignorance – almost *is* the revelation of ignorance. Our knowledge of the world instructs us first of all that the world is greater than our knowledge of it. To those who rejoice in the abundance and intricacy of Creation, this is a source of joy, as it is to those who rejoice in freedom. ('The future comes only by surprise,' we say, '– thank God!') To those would-be solvers of 'the human problem', who hope for knowledge equal to (capable of controlling) the world, it is a source of unremitting defeat and bewilderment. The evidence is overwhelming that knowledge does not solve 'the human problem'. Indeed, the evidence overwhelmingly suggests – with Genesis – that knowledge *is* the problem. Or perhaps we should say instead that all our problems tend to gather under two questions about knowledge: having the ability and desire to know, how and what should we learn? and having learned, how and for what should we use what we know?

One thing we do know, that we dare not forget, is that better solutions than ours have at times been made by people with much less information than we have. We know too, from the study of agriculture, that the same information, tools and techniques that in one farmer's hands will ruin land, in another's will save and improve it.

This is not a recommendation of ignorance. To know nothing, after all, is no more possible than to know enough. I am only proposing that knowledge, like everything else, has its place, and that we need urgently now to *put* it in its place. If we want to know and cannot help knowing, then let us learn as fully and accurately as we decently can. But let us at the same time abandon our superstitious beliefs about knowledge: that it is ever sufficient; that it can of itself solve problems; that it is intrinsically good; that it can be used objectively or disinterestedly. Let us acknowledge that the objective or disinterested researcher is always on the side that pays best. And let us give up our forlorn pursuit of the 'informed decision'.

The 'informed decision', I suggest, is as fantastical

a creature as the 'disinterested third party' and the 'objective observer'. Or it is if by 'informed' we mean 'supported by sufficient information'. A great deal of our public life, and certainly the most expensive part of it, rests on the assumed possibility of decisions so informed. Examination of private life, however, affords no comfort whatsoever to that assumption. It is simply true that we do not and cannot *know* enough to make any important decision.

Take Marriage as an Instance

Of this dilemma we can take marriage as an instance, for as a condition marriage reveals the insufficiency of knowledge, and as an institution it suggests the possibility that decisions can be informed in another way that *is* sufficient, or approximately so. I take it as an axiom that one cannot know enough to get married, any more than one can predict a surprise. The only people who possess information sufficient to their vows are widows and widowers – who do not know enough to *re*-marry.

I have been told several times by people younger than I am that people of their age cannot make marriage like some people of my age. I have always replied that I understood what they meant, avoiding – appropriately, I hope – an application of my general opinion to anyone's particular case. But I confess, in general, that what I understood them to mean has troubled me, for I think they can have meant one of only two things: that marriage is too good for them, and they were unwilling to bring it down to the level of their imperfections; or that they were too good for marriage, unwilling to limit themselves by the foreswearings that marriage so unexceptionally imposes.

124

What is not so well understood now as perhaps it used to be is that marriage is made in an inescapable condition of loneliness and ignorance, to which it, or something like it, is the only possible answer. Perhaps this is so hard to understand because now the most noted solutions are mechanical solutions, which are often exactly suited to mechanical problems. But we are humans – which means that we not only *have* problems, but *are* problems. Marriage is not as nicely trimmed to its purpose as a bottle-stopper; it is a not entirely possible solution to a not entirely soluble problem. And this is true of the other human connections. We can commit ourselves fully to anything – a place, a discipline, a life's work, a child, a family, a community, a faith, a friend – only in the same poverty of knowledge, the same ignorance of result, the same self-subordination, the same final forsaking of other possibilities. Marriage is an institution and requires vows *because* it can be made only in the eclipse of what we call information, and in the impossibility of what we call 'informed decisions'.

All our commitments are like this. We do not know enough to make them, and whether or not we have made them publicly with vows, we know that they cannot be unmade without penalties. If we must make these so final commitments without sufficient information, then what *can* inform our decisions?

In spite of the obvious dangers of the word, we must say first that love can inform them. This, of course, though probably necessary, is not safe. What parent, faced with a child who is in love and going to get married, has not been filled with mistrust and fear – and justly so. We who were lovers before we were parents know what a fraudulent justifier love can be. We know that people stay married for different reasons than those for which they get married, and that the later reasons will have to be discovered. Which, of course, is not to say that the later reasons may not confirm the earlier ones; it is to say only that the earlier ones must wait for confirmation.

Character and Culture

But our decisions can also be informed – our loves both limited and strengthened – by those patterns of value and restraint, principle and expectation, memory, familiarity and understanding that, inwardly, add up to *character* and, outwardly, to *culture*. Because of these patterns, and only because of them, we are not alone in the bewilderments of the human condition and human love, but have the company and the comfort of the best of our kind, living and dead. These patterns constitute a knowledge far different from the kind I have been talking about. It is a kind of knowledge that includes information, but is never the same as information. Indeed, if we study the paramount documents of our culture, we will see that this second kind of knowledge invariably implies, and often explicitly imposes, limits upon the first kind: some possibilities must not be explored; some things must not be learned. If we want to get safely home, there are certain seductive songs we must not turn aside for, some sacred things we must not meddle with:

> Great captain,
> a fair wind and the honey lights of home
> are all you seek. But anguish lies ahead;
> the god who thunders on the land prepares it . . .
> One narrow strait may take you through his blows:
> denial of yourself, restraint of shipmates.

This theme, of course, is dominant in biblical tradition, but the theme itself and its modern inversion can be handily understood by a comparison of this speech of Tiresias to Odysseus, in Homer, with Tennyson's romantic Ulysses who proposes, like a genetic engineer or an atomic scientist,

> To follow knowledge like a sinking star,
> Beyond the utmost bound of human thought.

Obviously, unlike Homer's Odysseus, Tennyson's Ulysses is said to come from Dante, and he does resemble Dante's Ulysses pretty exactly – the critical difference being that Dante thought this Ulysses a madman and a fool, and brings down upon his Tennysonian speech to his sailors one of the swiftest anti-climaxes in literature. The real – the human – knowledge is understood as implying and imposing limits, much as marriage does, and these limits are understood to belong necessarily to the definition of a human being.

In all this talk about marriage I have not forgotten that I am supposed to be talking about agriculture. I am going to talk directly about agriculture in a minute, but I want to insist that I have been talking about it indirectly all along, for the analogy between marriage-making and farm-making, marriage-keeping and farm-keeping, is nearly exact. I have talked about marriage as a way of talking about farming because marriage, as a human artifact, has been more carefully understood than farming. The analogy between them is so close, for one thing, because they join us to time in nearly the same way. In talking about time, I will begin to talk directly about farming, but as I do so, you will be aware, I hope, that I am talking indirectly about marriage.

When people speak with confidence of the longevity

of diminishing agricultural sources – as when they speak of their good intentions about nuclear power – they are probably not just being gullible or thoughtless. They are likely to be speaking from belief in several tenets of industrial optimism: that life is long, but time and work are short; that every problem will be solved by a 'technological breakthrough' before it enlarges to catastrophe; that *any* problem can be solved in a hurry by large applications of urgent emotion, information and money. It is regrettable that these assumptions should risk correction by disaster when they could be cheaply and safely overturned by the study of any agriculture that has proved durable.

To the farmer, Emerson said, 'The landscape is an armoury of powers . . .' As he meant it, the statement may be true, but the metaphor is ill-chosen, for the powers of a landscape are available to human use in nothing like so simple a way as are the powers of an armoury. Or let us say, anyhow, that the preparations needed for the taking up of agricultural powers are more extensive and complex than those usually thought necessary for the taking up of arms. And let us add that the motives are, or ought to be, significantly different.

Farming in Love

Arms are taken up in hate, but it has not been uncharacteristic for a farmer's connection to a farm to begin in love. This has not always been so ignorant a love as it sometimes is now; but always, no matter what one's agricultural experience may have been, one's connection to a newly-bought farm will begin in love that is more or less ignorant. One loves the place because present appearances recommend it, and because

128

they suggest possibilities irresistibly imaginable. One's head, like a lover's, grows full of visions. One walks over the premises, saying, 'If this were mine, I'd make a permanent pasture here; here is where I'd plant an orchard; here is where I'd dig a pond.' These visions are the usual stuff of unfulfilled love, and induce wakefulness at night.

When one buys the farm and moves there to live, something different begins. Thoughts begin to be translated into acts. Truth begins to intrude with its matter-of-fact. One's work may be defined in part by one's visions, but it is defined in part too by problems, which the work leads to and reveals. And daily life, work and problems gradually alter the visions. It invariably turns out, I think, that one's first vision of one's place was to some extent an imposition on it. But if one's sight is clear and if one stays on and works well, one's love gradually responds to the place as it really is, and one's visions gradually imagine possibilities that are really in it. Vision, possibility, work and life – *all* have changed by mutual correction. Correct discipline, given enough time, gradually removes one's self from one's line of sight. One works to better purpose then and makes fewer mistakes, because at last one sees where one is. Two human possibilities of the highest order thus come within reach: what one wants can become the same as what one has; and one's knowledge can cause respect for what one knows.

'Correct discipline' and 'enough time' are inseparable notions. Correct discipline cannot be hurried, for it is both the knowledge of what ought to be done and the willingness to do it – *all* of it, properly. The good worker will not suppose that good work can be made properly answerable to haste, urgency or even emergency. But the good worker knows too that, after it is done, work requires yet more time to prove its worth.

One must stay to experience and study and understand it by living with it, and then correct it, if necessary, by longer living and more work. It won't do to correct mistakes made in one place by moving to another place, as has been the common fashion in America, or by adding on another place, as is the fashion in any sort of 'growth economy'. Seen this way, questions about farming become inseparable from questions about propriety of scale. A farm can be too big for a farmer to husband properly or pay proper attention to. Distraction is inimical to correct discipline, and enough time is beyond the reach of anyone who has too much to do. But we must go farther and see that propriety of scale is invariably associated with propriety of another kind: an understanding and acceptance of the human place in the order of Creation – a proper humility. There are some things the arrogant mind does not see; it is blinded by its vision of what it desires. It does not see what is already there; it never sees the forest that precedes the farm, or the farm that precedes the shopping centre; it will never understand that America was 'discovered' by the Indians. It is the properly humbled mind in its proper place that sees truly, because – to give only one reason – it sees details.

And the good farmer understands that further limits are imposed upon haste by Nature which, except for an occasional storm or earthquake, is in no hurry either. In the processes of most concern to agriculture – the building and preserving of fertility – Nature is never in a hurry. During the last eighteen years, for example, I have been working at the restoration of a once exhausted hillside. Its scars are now healed over, though still visible, and this year it has provided abundant pasture, more than in any year since we have owned it. But to make it as good as it is now has taken eighteen years. If I had been a millionaire or if my family had been starving, it would still have taken eighteen years. It can be better than it now is, but that will take longer. For it to live fully in its own possibility, as it did before bad use ran it down, may take hundreds of years.

Thinking through Hundreds of Years and Farming

But to think of the human use of a piece of land as continuing through hundreds of years, we must greatly complicate our understanding of agriculture. Let us start a job of farming on a given place – say an initially fertile hillside in the Kentucky River Valley – and construe it through time.

1. To begin using this hillside for agricultural production – pasture or crop – is a matter of a year's work. This is work in the present tense, adequately comprehended by conscious intention and by the first sort of knowledge I talked about: information available to the farmer's memory and built into his methods, tools and crop and livestock species. Understood in its present tense, the work does not reveal its value except insofar as the superficial marks of craftsmanship may be seen and judged. But excellent workmanship, as with a breaking plough, may prove as damaging as bad workmanship. The work has not revealed its connections to the place or to the worker. These connections are revealed in time.

2. To live on the hillside and use it for a lifetime gives the annual job of work a past and a future. To live on the hillside and use it without diminishing its fertility or wasting it by erosion still requires conscious intention and information, but now we must say *good* intention and *good* (that is, correct) information, re-

sulting in *good* work. And to these we must now add
character: the sort of knowledge that might properly
be called familiarity, and the affections, habits, values
and virtues (conscious and unconscious) that would
preserve good care and good work through hard times.

3. For human life to continue on the hillside through
successive generations requires good use, good work,
all along. For in any agricultural place that will waste
or erode – and all will – bad work does not permit
'muddling through'; sooner or later it ends human life.
Human continuity is virtually synonymous with good
farming, and good farming obviously must outlast the
life of any good farmer. For it to do this, in addition
to the preceding requirements, we must have *community*. Without community, the good work of a single
farmer or a single family will not mean much or last
long. For good farming to last, it must occur in a good
farming community – that is, a neighbourhood of
people who know one another, who understand their
mutual dependencies, and who place a proper value on
good farming. In its cultural aspect, the community is
an order of memories preserved consciously in instructions, songs and stories, and both consciously and unconsciously in *ways*. A healthy culture holds preserving
knowledge *in place* for a *long* time. That is, the essential wisdom accumulates in the community much as
fertility builds in the soil. In both, death becomes
potentiality.

People are joined to the land by work. Land, work,
people and community are all comprehended in the
idea of culture. These connections cannot be understood or described by information – so many resources
to be transformed by so many workers into so many
products for so many consumers – because they are not
quantitative. We can understand them only after we
acknowledge that they should be harmonious – that a

society must be either shapely and saving or shapeless and destructive. To presume to describe land, work, people and community by information, by quantities, seems invariably to throw them into competition with one another. Work is understood to exploit the land, the people to exploit their work, the community to exploit its people. And then, instead of land, work, people and community, we have the industrial categories of resources, labour, management, consumers and government. We have exchanged harmony for an interminable fuss, and the work of culture for the timed and harried labour of an industrial economy.

But let me bring these notions to the trial of a more particular example.

Wes Jackson and Marty Bender of the Land Institute have recently worked out a comparison between the energy economy of a farm using draft horses for most of its field work with that of an identical farm using tractors. This is a project a generation overdue, of the greatest interest and importance: in short, necessary. And the results will be shocking to those who assume a direct proportion between fossil fuel combustion and human happiness.

These results, however, have not fully explained one fact that Wes and Marty had before them at the start of their analysis and that was still running ahead of them at the end: that in the last twenty-five or thirty years, the Old Order Amish, who use horses for farmwork, doubled their population and stayed in farming, whereas in the same period millions of mechanized farmers were driven out. The reason that this is not adequately explained by analysis of the two energy economies, I believe, is that the problem is by its nature beyond the reach of analysis of any kind. The real or whole reason must be impossibly complicated, having to do with Nature, culture, religion, family and community life, as well as with agricultural methodology and economies. What I think we are up against is an unresolvable difference between thought and action, thought and life.

What works *poorly* in agriculture – monoculture, for instance, or annual accounting – can be pretty fully explained, because what works poorly is invariably some oversimplifying *thought* that subjugates Nature, people and culture. What works well defies explanation because it involves an order which in both magnitude and complexity is ultimately incomprehensible.

Here, then, is a prime example of the futility of a dependence on information. We cannot contain what contains us, or comprehend what comprehends us. Yeats said that 'Man can embody truth but he cannot know it.' The part, that is, cannot comprehend the whole, though it can stand for it (and by it). Synec-doche is possible, and its possibility implies the possi-bility of harmony between part and whole. If we cannot work on the basis of sufficient information, then we have to work on the basis of an understanding of har-mony. That, I take it, is what Sir Albert Howard and Wes Jackson mean when they tell us that we must study and emulate on our farms the natural integrities that precede and support agriculture.

The study of Amish agriculture, like the study of *any* durable agriculture, suggests that we live in sequences of patterns that are formally analogous. These se-quences are probably hierarchical, at least in the sense that some patterns are more comprehensive than others; they tend to arrange themselves like inter-nest-ing bowls – though any attempt to represent their order visually will over-simplify it.

And so we must suspect that Amish horse-powered farms work well, not because – or not *just* because – horses are energy-efficient, but because they are living creatures, and therefore fit harmoniously into a pattern of relationships that are necessarily biological, and that rhyme analogically from ecosystem to crop, from field to farmer. In other words, ecosystem, farm, field, crop, horse, farmer, family and community are in certain critical ways *like* one another. They are, for instance, all related to health and fertility or reproductivity in about the same way. The health and fertility of each involves and is involved in the health and fertility of all.

It goes without saying that tools can be introduced into this agricultural and ecological order without jeopardizing it – but only up to a certain kind, scale and power. To introduce a tractor into it, as the historical record now seems virtually to prove, is to begin its destruction. The tractor has been so destructive, I think, because it is *unlike* anything else in the agricultural order, and so it breaks the essential harmony. With the tractor comes dependence on an energy supply that lies not only off the farm, but outside agriculture and outside biological cycles and integrities. With the tractor, both farm and farmer become 'resources' of the industrial economy, which always exploits its resources.

We would be wrong, of course, to say that anyone who farms with a tractor is a bad farmer. That is not true. What we must say, however, is that once a tractor is introduced into the pattern of a farm, certain necessary restraints and practices, once implicit in technology, must now reside in the character and consciousness of the farmer – at the same time that the economic pressure to cast off restraint and good practice has been greatly increased.

In a society addicted to facts and figures, anyone trying to speak for agricultural *harmony* is inviting trouble. The first trouble is in trying to say what har-

135

mony is. It cannot be reduced to facts and figures – though the lack of it can. It is not very visibly a function. Perhaps we can only say what it may be like. It may, for instance, be like sympathetic vibration: 'The A string of a violin . . . is designed to vibrate most readily at about 440 vibrations per second: the note A. If that same note is played loudly not on the violin but near it, the violin A string may hum in sympathy.' This may have a practical exemplification in the craft of the mud daubers which, as they trowel mud into their nest walls, hum to it, or at it, communicating a vibration that makes it easier to work, thus mastering their material by a kind of song. Perhaps the hum of the mud dauber only activates that anciently-perceived likeness between all creatures and the earth of which they are made. For as common wisdom holds, like *speaks to* like. And harmony always involves such specificities of form as in the mud dauber's song and its nest, whereas information accumulates indiscriminately, like noise.

Of course, in the order of creatures, humanity is a special case. Humans are not involved in harmony naturally, like mud daubers. For humans, harmony is always a human product, an artifact, and if they do not know how to make it and choose to make it, then they do not have it. And so I suggest that, for humans, the harmony I am talking about may bear an inescapable likeness to what we know as moral law – or that, for humans, moral law is a significant part of the notation of ecological and agricultural harmony. A great many people seem to have voted for information as a safe substitute for virtue, but this ignores – among much else – the need to prepare humans to live short lives in the fact of long work and long time.

Perhaps it is only when we focus our minds on our machines that times seems short. Time is always running out for machines. They shorten our work, in a

sense popularly approved, by simplifying it and speed-
ing it up, but our work perishes quickly in them too as
they wear out and are discarded. For the living Creation, on the other hand, time is always coming. It is
running out for the farm built on the industrial pattern;
the industrial farm burns fertility as it burns fuel. For
the farm built into the pattern of living things, as an
analogue of forest or prairie, time is a bringer of gifts.
These gifts may be welcomed and cared for. To some
extent they may be expected. Only within strict limits
are they the result of human intention and knowledge.
They cannot in the usual sense be made. Only in the
short term of industrial accounting can they be thought
simply earnable. Over the real length of human time,
to be earned they must be deserved.

From this rather wandering excursion I arrive at two
conclusions.

The first is that the modern prototype of an intelligent person is probably wrong. The prototypical modern intelligence seems to be that of the Quiz Kid – a
human shape barely discernable in a fluff of facts. It is
understood that everything must be justified by facts,
and facts are offered in justification of *everything*. If it
is a fact that soil erosion is now a critical problem in
American agriculture, then more facts will indicate that
it is not as bad as it *could* be and that Iowa will continue
to have topsoil for as long as seventy more years. If
facts show that some people are undernourished in
America, further facts reveal that we should all be glad
we do not live in India. This, of course, is machine
thought.

To think better, to think like the best humans, we
are probably going to have to learn again to judge a
person's intelligence, not by the ability to recite facts,
but by the good order or harmoniousness of his or her
surroundings. We must suspect that any statistical jus-

tification of ugliness and violence is a revelation of stupidity. As an earlier student of agriculture put it: 'The intelligent man, however unlearned, may be known by his surroundings, and by the care of his horse, if he is fortunate enough to own one.'

My second conclusion is that any public programme to preserve land or produce food is hopeless if it does not tend to right the balance between numbers of people and acres of land, and to encourage long-term, stable connections between families and small farms. It could be argued that our nation has never made an effort in this direction that was knowledgeable enough or serious enough. It is certain that no such effort, in America, has ever succeeded. The typical American farm is probably sold and remade – often as part of a larger farm – at least every generation. Farms that have been passed to the second generation of the same family are unusual. Farms that have passed to the third generation are rare.

But our crying need is for an agriculture in which the typical farm would be farmed by the third generation of the same family. It would be wrong to try to say exactly what kind of agriculture that would be, but it may be allowable to suggest that certain good possibilities would be enhanced.

The most important of those possibilities would be the lengthening of memory. Previous mistakes, failures and successes would be remembered. The land would not have to pay the cost of a trial-and-error education for every new owner. A half-century or more of the farm's history would be living memory, and its present health could be measured against its own past – something exceedingly difficult *outside* of living memory.

A second possibility is that the land would not be over-worked to pay for itself at full value with every new owner.

A third possibility would be that, having some confidence in family continuity in place, present owners would have future owners not only in supposition but *in sight*, and so would take good care of the land, not for the sake of something so abstract as 'the future' or 'posterity', but out of particular love for living children and grandchildren.

A fourth possibility is that having the past so immediately in memory, and the future so tangibly in prospect, the human establishment on the land would grow more permanent by the practice of better carpentry and masonry. People who remembered long and well would see the folly of rebuilding their barns every generation or two and of building new fences every twenty years.

A fifth possibility would be the development of the concept of *enough*. Only long memory can answer, for a given farm or locality: How much land is enough? How much work is enough? How much livestock and crop production is enough? How much power is enough?

A sixth possibility is that of local culture. Who could say what that would be? As members of a society based on the exploitation of its own temporariness, we probably should not venture a guess. But we can perhaps speak with a little competence of how it would begin. It would not be imported from critically approved cultures elsewhere. It would not come from watching certified classics on TV. It would begin in work and love. People at work in communities three generations old would know that their bodies renewed time and again the movements of other bodies, living and dead, known and loved, remembered and loved, in the same shops, houses and fields. That, of course, is a description of a kind of community dance. And such a dance is perhaps the best way we have to describe harmony.

VII

Wild, Sacred, Good Land
Saving the Little Waterhole We Sing By

Gary Snyder

I live on land in the Sierra Nevada of California, continent of Turtle Island, which is just barely good, somewhat wild and potentially sacred. In my work of recent
years at home developing a mountain farmstead, and
in cities attending environmental political meetings, or
farther afield studying the problems of indigenous
peoples on the land, I find each of these ways of speaking of land regularly emerging. In examining these
three categories, perhaps we can get some further insights into the deeper problems of rural habitation,
subsistence living, wilderness preservation, Third and
Fourth World resistance to the appetites of industrial
civilization, and what sort of spirit it takes to save the
planet. All three ways of speaking of land are respectful, though they contain within them differences; and
all are implicitly concerned with Right Livelihood. Our
present dominant industrial economies can lead only
to the land – all over the planet – becoming exhausted,
over-developed or desecrated. In a word – a CIA word
– 'de-stabilized'.

Gary Snyder

I

Wild, in its wider meaning, refers to all of unmanipulated, unmanaged natural habitat. Much of precivilized wild planetary space was hospitable to humans – rich rainforests, grasslands covered with bison, mammoths or pronghorns, and teeming seacoasts. Near-climax, high biomass, perennially productive, such a place is an essential expression of biological nature.

For non-agricultural people 'wild' would also be 'good'. Even inhospitable mountain or desert terrain may provide special plants or animals of unique value. Concepts of 'sacred land' are found widely in nonagricultural societies, and, without stopping right yet to examine the nature of the numinosity of sacrosanct spots, we know that sacred sites are in almost every case also wild. In many instances the same place might be considered simultaneously wild, good and sacred.

In agricultural societies 'good land' is narrowed to mean land productive of a much smaller range of favoured cultivars, and thus the opposite of wild: 'cultivated'. Grassland or woodland hunting and gathering peoples who look over the fence into farming territory see cultivated fields as far from good. To their eyes, a religious spirit that rejoices in the fertility of all Nature is replaced by a focus only on crops. Members of the Bos and Sus clans, which are interesting animals in the wild, are tamed and transformed into sluggish meat-making machines. The 'field' consciousness of the hunters' and gatherers' wide-ranging daily world is supplanted by an inner map made up of highly productive nodes (cleared fields) connected by lines (trails through the forest). Hence, 'linear'.

In civilized agrarian states the term 'sacred' is sometimes applied to ritually cultivated land or temple fields; it can also refer to remnant groves or grottos where gods are thought still to linger. The wild has become possibly demonic, and the term 'cultivation' is extended to describe a kind of training in lore and manners that guarantees membership in an élite class. It can even be used to describe religious *askesis*, spiritual training. A holy man is a super-cultivated man by this metaphor. The thought that wild might also be sacred returns to the Occident only with the Romantic movement. This re-appreciation of nature projects a rather vague sense of the sacred, however. It is only from very old place-centred cultures that we hear of sacred groves, sacred land, in a context of genuine belief and practice.

In North America and Australia the original inhabitants are facing the latest round of incursions into their remotest territories. These reservations or reserves were left in their use because the dominant society thought the arctic tundra or arid desert 'no good'. The people of Australia, Alaska and elsewhere are vigorously fighting to keep logging or oil exploration or uranium mining out of some of their landscapes, and not only for the reason that it is actually their own land, but also because some places in it are sacred.

So a very cogent and current political issue rises around the question of the possible sacredness of certain spots. I was at the University of Montana in the spring of '82 on a programme with Russell Means, the AIM founder and activist, who was trying to get support for the Yellow Thunder Camp of Lakota and other India people of the Black Hills, on what is currently called Forest Service land. They wish to block further expansion of mining into the Black Hills. They argue that the particular piece they are on is not only ancestral land but is sacred.

Governor Jerry Brown during his term in the State of California created the Native American Heritage

Commission specifically for California Indians, and the commission identified a number of Elders who were charged with the task of locating and protecting sacred sites and graves in California. This would avoid in advance confrontations between landowners or public land managers. It was a sensitive move, and though barely comprehensible to the white voters, it sent a ripple of appreciation through all the native communities. The white Christian founders of the US were probably not considering American Indian religions when they guaranteed freedom of religion, but interpretations by the courts and the passage of the American Indian Religious Freedom Act of 1978 have gradually come to give native practices some real status. 'Sacred' virtually becomes a new 'land-use category'.

Yet even as I write this, February 1983, it seems possible that the Act is worthless, and that the Government and the courts have no understanding of the religious use and veneration of wild land. In northern California, in the Six Rivers National Forest, a historic confrontation is in the making. The court has given the go-ahead, over the recommendations of both anthropologists and Indians, to the construction of a road through ancient, impeccably practised, sacred high-mountain land. This is the Chimney Rock, Doctor Rock area of the Blue Creek drainage. The Tolowa, Yurok and Karuk people have considered this region the centre of their religious practice since the Dreamtime. The Forest Service, however, can include it in their 'Timber Management Plan', and a judge can declare that if the Forest Service has 'studied the situation', that's enough; it bears no obligation to respect the beliefs and traditions of the living native people of the area. Wilderness activists and Indians will be standing together in trying literally to block this road.

II

In the hunting-and-gathering way of life the whole territory of a given group is fairly equally experienced by everyone. It will be known for its many plant communities, high and low terrain, good views, odd-shaped rocks, dangerous spots, and places made special by myth or story. There are places where women go for seclusion or to give birth, places the bodies of the dead are taken to. There are spots where young girls or young boys are called to for special instruction. Some places in this territory become numinous – loaded with meaning and power. This has happened to all of us. The memories of such spots are very long.

I was in Australia in the fall of 1981 at the invitation of the Australian Aboriginal Arts Board doing some teaching, poetry readings, and workshops with Aboriginal leaders and children. Much of the time I was in the central Australian desert south and west of Alice Springs, first into Pitjantjara tribal territory, and then 300 miles northwest into Pintubi tribal territory. The Aboriginal people in the central desert all still speak their languages. Their religion is fairly intact, and most young men are still initiated at 14, even the ones who go to high school at Alice Springs. They leave the high school with the co-operation of the school authorities for a year, and are taken out into the bush to learn bush ways on foot, to master the lore of landscapes and plants and animals, and finally to undergo initiation.

I was travelling by truck over dirt track west from Alice in the company of a Pintubi elder named Jimmy Tjungurrayi. As we rolled along the dusty road, sitting in the bed of a pickup, he began to speak very rapidly to me. He was talking about a mountain over there, telling me a story about some wallabies that came to that mountain in the dreamtime and got into some kind of mischief there with some lizard girls. He had hardly finished that then he started in on another story about another hill over here and another story over here. I couldn't keep up. I realized after about half an hour of this that these were tales to be told while *walking*, and that I was experiencing a speeded-up version of what might be leisurely said over several days of foot-travel. Mr Tjungurrayi felt graciously compelled to share a body of lore with me by virtue of the very fact that I was there.

So remember a time when you journeyed on foot over hundreds of miles, walking fast and often travelling at night, travelling night-long and napping in the acacia shade during the day, and these stories were told to you as you went. In your travels with an older person you were given a map you could memorize, full of the lore and song, and also practical information. Off by yourself you could sing those songs to bring yourself back. And you could travel to a place that you'd never been, carrying only songs you had learned.

We made camp at a waterhole called Ilpili and rendezvoused with a number of Pintubi people from the surrounding desert country. Through the night until one or two in the morning, Jimmy Tjungurrayi and the other older men sat and sang a cycle of journey songs, walking through a space of desert in imagination and song. They stopped between songs and would hum a phrase or two and then would argue a bit about the words and then would start again, and someone would defer to another person and would let him start. Jimmy explained to me that they have so many cycles of journey songs they can't quite remember them all, and that they have to be constantly rehearsing them. Night after night they say, 'What will we sing tonight? Let's sing the walk up to Darwin.' They'll start out and argue their way along through it, and stop when it gets too late to go any further. I asked Jimmy, 'Well, how far did you get last night?' He said, 'Well, we got two-thirds of the way to Darwin.' This is a way to transmit information about vast terrain which is obviously very effective and doesn't require writing. Some of the places thus defined will be presented as sacred, as well.

One day, driving near Ilpili, we stopped the truck and Jimmy and three other elderly gentlemen got out and said, 'We'll take you out to see a sacred place here.' They turned to the young boys and said, 'Uninitiated boys can't go there.' As we climbed the hill, these ordinarily cheery and loud-talking Aboriginal men began to drop their voices. As we got higher up the hill they were speaking in whispers, their whole manner changed. They said, 'Now we are coming close', entirely in whispers. Then they got on their hands and knees and crawled. We crawled up the last 200 feet, over a little rise into an area of severe broken and odd rock shapes. They whispered to us very profoundly, in a state of great respect and awe, and told us a little of what was there and its story. Then we all backed away. We got back down the hill and at a certain point stood and walked. At another point voices rose. Back at the truck, everybody was talking loud again and no more mention was made of the sacred place.

Very powerful. Very much in mind. We learned later it was also a place where young men were taken for instruction and for initiation – not full-scale initiation, but some little initiations that are of special instruction.

So the nature of the 'sacred place' in Australia began to define itself as special rocks, beautiful, steep defiles where two cliffs almost meet with maybe just a little sandbed between, a place where many parrots are nesting in the rock walls, or a place where a blade of rock stood on end balancing, 30 feet tall, by a waterhole. Each of them was out of the ordinary, a little fantastic even, and all were places of teaching. Often they had pictographs left by far-past human ancestors. In some cases they were also what are called 'dreaming spots' for certain totem ancestors. 'Dreaming' or 'Dreamtime' refers to a time of creation which is not in the past but which is here right now. It's the mode of eternally creative now-ness as contrasted with the mode of cause-and-effect in time, the main place that modern people live and within which we imagine history, progress and evolution to take place. The totem dreaming place is first of all special to the people of that totem, who sometimes make pilgrimages there; second it is sacred to the honey-ants (say) which actually live there. There are a lot of honey-ants there. Third, it's like a little Platonic cave of ideal honey-ant forms. (I'm imagining this now. I'm trying to explain what all these things seem to be.) It's the archetypal honey-ant spot. In fact, it's optimal honey-ant habitat. A green parrot dreaming place, with the tracks of the ancestors going across the landscape and stopping at the green parrot dreaming place, is a perfect green parrot nesting spot. So the sacredness comes together with a sense of optimal habitat of certain kinfolk that we have out there: the wallabies, red kangaroo, bush turkey, lizards. Robert Bliney sums it up this way: 'The land itself was their chapel and their shrines were hills and creeks and their religious relics were animals, plants and birds. Thus the migrations of Aboriginals, though spurred by economic need, were also always pilgrimages.' 'Good' (productive of much life), 'wild' (naturally) and, in these cases, 'sacred' were indeed one.

This way of life is going on right now, threatened by Japanese uranium mining, large-scale copper mining, and petroleum exploration throughout the deserts. The issue of sacredness is a very real political question, so much so that the Australian Bureau of Aboriginal Affairs has hired some bilingual anthropologists and bush people to work with elders of the different tribes to identify sacred sites and map them. Everyone hopes that the Australian government really means this: to declare certain areas off-limits before any exploratory team ever gets near them. This process is spurred by the fact that there have already been some confrontations over oil exploration in the Kimberley region. This was at Nincoomba. The people very firmly stood their ground and made human lines in front of bulldozers and drilling rigs, and won the support of the Australian public to their side. Since then the Australian government is being very careful. In Australian land ownership, mineral rights are always reserved to 'the Crown' so that even a private ranch is subject to mining. To consider sacred land as a special category in Australia is a very interesting and advanced mode, at least in theory. Recently a 'registered sacred site' was bulldozed near Alice Springs, supposedly on instructions of a government land minister, and this is in the relatively benign Federal Government jurisdiction! The State of Queensland is a mini-fascist nation to itself, favoured by emigrants from white South Africa.

III

The original inhabitants of Japan, the Ainu, can see a whole system sacred. Their term, 'iworu', means 'field', with implications of watershed, plant and animal life, and spirit force. They can speak of the *iworu* of the great brown bear. By that they mean the mountain habitat and watershed territory in which the brown bear is dominant. They also speak of the *iworu* of the salmon, which means the lower watersheds with all their tributaries and the plant communities along those valleys that focus on the streams where salmon run. The bear field, the deer field, the salmon field, the orca (killer whale) field. To give a little picture of how this world works, a human house is up a valley by a stream, facing east. In the centre of the house is the fire. The sunshine streams through the eastern door each morning to contact the fire-goddess: the sun-goddess contacts her sister the fire-goddess in the firepit. They communicate for a moment. One must not step across the sunbeams that shine in the morning on the firepit; that would be breaking their contact.

Food comes from the inner mountains and from the deeps of the sea. The lord of the deeps of the sea is Orca or Killer Whale, the lord of the inner mountains is Bear. Bear sends his friends the deer down to visit us. Killer Whale sends his friends the salmon to visit us up the streams. When they come to visit us we kill them, to enable them to get out of their fur or scale coats, and then we entertain them because they love music. We sing songs to them and we eat them. Having been delighted by the songs they heard, they return to the deep sea and to the inner mountains, and they report to the deep sea and to the inner mountains and they report to their spirit friends there, 'We had a wonderful time with the human beings. There's lots to eat, lots to drink and they played music for us.' The other ones say, 'Oh, let's go visit the human beings.' If the people do not neglect the proper hospitality, the music and manners, when entertaining their deer or salmon or wild plant-food visitors, the beings will be reborn and return over and over. This is a sort of spiritual game-management.

The Ainu were probably the original inhabitants of all of Japan. They certainly left many place names behind and many traces on the landscape. Modern Japan is another sort of example: a successful industrialized country, with remnants of sacred land-consciousness still intact. There are *Shinto* shrines throughout Japan. *Shinto*: 'the way of the spirits'. By 'spirits', the Japanese mean exactly what almost all people of the world have always meant by spirits; formless little powers present in everything to some degree but intensified in power and in presence in outstanding objects, such as large, interestingly twisted rocks, very old trees, or large, beautiful waterfalls. Anomalies and beauties of the landscape are all signs of *kami*: spirit power, spirit presence, energy. The greatest of all the *kami*, or spirit forces, in Japan is Mount Fuji; the name Fuji is now thought to be an old Ainu place name of the fire-goddess. All of Mount Fuji is a Shinto shrine, the largest in the nation, from well below timber line all the way to the summit.

Shinto got a bad name during the '30s and World War II because the Japanese government created a 'state Shinto' in the service of militarism and nationalism. Long before the rise of any state, the islands of Japan were studded with little shrines – *jinja* or *miya* – that reflect neolithic village culture. Even in the midst of the enormous onrushing industrial energy of the current system, one thing that is still untouchable is shrine lands. It would make your hair stand up to see how the Japanese will take bulldozers to a nice slope of pines to level it for a new development. When the New Island was created in Kobe harbour, to become the second largest port in the world (after Rotterdam), it was raised on the bay bottom from dirt obtained by shaving down a range of hills ten miles south of the city and barging it to the site for 12 years. A steady stream of barges was carrying dirt off giant conveyor belts, which totally removed land two ranges back from the coast. That area was converted into a housing development. With such capacities we can duly appreciate that shrine land is untouchable. In the industrial world, it's not that 'nothing is sacred', but that the sacred is sacred and that's *all* that is sacred. We are grateful for this little bit of Japanese salvaged land because the rule in shrine lands is that you never cut anything, never maintain anything, never clear or thin anything. No hunting, no fishing, no thinning, no burning, no stopping of burning. Thus there are pockets of climax forests here and there, right inside the city, so that one can walk into a shrine and be in the presence of 800-year-old cryptomeria trees. Without them we wouldn't know what Japanese forests might have been. But such compartmentalization is not healthy: in this model, some land you save, like a virgin priestess, some you overwork endlessly, like a wife, and some you brutally, publicly reshape, like a whore. 'Good', 'wild' and 'sacred' couldn't be farther apart.

IV

Europe and the Middle East inherit from neolithic and paleolithic times many shrines. The most sacred spot in all Europe was perhaps the caves of southern France, in the Pyrenees. We shall say that they were the great shrines of 20,000 years ago, the centre of a religious complex in which the animals were brought underground. Maybe a dreaming place. Maybe a thought that the archetypal animal forms were thereby stored under the earth, a way of keeping animals from becoming extinct. But many species did become extinct. Most became so during the last two thousand years, victims of the *imperium* of civilization in its particularly destructive Western form. The degradation of wild habitat and extinction of species, the impoverishment and enslavement of rural people and subsistence economies, and the burning alive of Nature-worship traditions was perfected right within Europe. So French and English explorers of North America and then the early fur traders and hunters had no traditions from the culture they left behind that would urge them to look on wild land with reverence. They did find much that was awe-inspiring, actually, and some joined the Indians and the land, and became people of place. These few almost forgotten exceptions were overwhelmed by fur trade entrepreneurs and, later, farmers. Yet many kept joining the Indians in fact or in style, grieving for a wilderness they saw shrinking away. In the Far East or Europe, a climax forest or a prairie and all the splendid creatures that live there is a tale from the neolithic. In the western United States that was our grandmothers' world. For many of us this loss, without intellectualization or question, is a source of grief. For native Americans, this loss is a loss of land, life and culture.

It is of course not evil to, as Thoreau did, 'make the soil say beans' – to cause it to be productive to our own notion – but we must also ask: what does Mother Nature do best here, when left to her own long strategies? This comes to asking: what would the climax vegetation of this spot be? For all land, however long-wasted and exploited, if left to Nature – the *tzuran*, 'self-so' of Taoism – will arrive at a point of balance between biological productivity and stability. A truly sophisticated post-industrial 'future primitive' agriculture will be asking: is there any way we can go *with* rather than against a natural tendency toward, say, deciduous hardwoods – or, as where I live, a mix of pine and oak with kitkitdizze ground-cover? Such a condition in many cases might be best for human interests too, and even in the short run.

Wesley Jackson's research indicates that a perennial and horticultural-based agriculture holds real promise for sustaining the locally appropriate communities of the future. This is acknowledging that the source of fertility ultimately is the 'wild'. It has been said, 'Good soil is good because of the wildness in it' – and, I would add, good land is not a gift from Jehovah or from a victorious king dividing up his spoils – 'Spanish land grants': royal/real estate – but a gift from *Gaia* herself; from the whole network.

It might be that almost all civilized agriculture has been on the wrong path from the beginning, relying on the monoculture of annuals. In *New Roots for Agriculture*, Wes Jackson develops this argument. I concur with his view, knowing that it raises even larger questions about civilization itself: a critique I have worked at elsewhere. Suffice it to say that the sorts of economic and social organization we invoke when we say 'civilization' can no longer be automatically accepted as useful models. To scrutinize civilization as Dr Stanley Diamond has in *The Search for the Primitive* is not, however, to negate all varieties of culture or cultivation.

The word 'cultivation' in civilization, harking to etymologies of 'till' and 'wheel about', generally implies a movement away from natural process. Both materially and psychologically, it is a matter of 'arresting succession, establishing monoculture'. Applied on the spiritual plane, this has meant austerities, obedience to religious authority, long, bookish scholarship, a dualistic devotionalism (sharply distinguishing 'creature and creator') and an over-riding metaphor of divinity being centralized, just as a secular ruler of a civilized state is at the centre – of wealth, of the metropole, of the political power: a king. The efforts entailed in such a spiritual practice are a sort of war against Nature, placing the human over the animal, the 'spiritual' over the human. The most sophisticated modern variety of this thought is possibly found in the works of Father Teilhard de Chardin, who claims a special evolutionary spiritual destiny for humanity under the name of higher consciousness. Some of the more extreme of these spiritual Darwinists would willingly leave the rest of earth-bound animal and plant life behind to enter a realm transcending biology. The anthropocentrism of some New Age thinkers is countered by the radical critique of the deep-ecology movement.

V

Yet there is such a thing as training. The natural world moves by process, and by complementarities of young and old, foolish and wise, ripe or green, raw or cooked. Animals too learn self-discipline and caution in the face of desire and availability. There is learning and training that goes with the grain of things. In early Chinese Taoism, training did not mean to cultivate the wildness out of oneself, but to do away with arbitrary and delusive conditioning – false social values distorting an essentially free and correct human nature. Buddhism takes a middle way, allowing that greed, hatred and stupidity are part of the given conditions of human nature, but seeing organized society, civilization, 'the world', as being a force that inflames, panders to or exploits these weaknesses in the fledgling human. Greed exposes the foolish person or the foolish chicken alike to the ever-watchful hawk of the food-web, and early impermanence. It's interesting to note that preliterate hunting-and-gathering cultures lived well by virtue of knowledge and a quiet sort of manipulation of systems. We know how the people of mesolithic Britain cleared or burned, in the valley of Thames, in a way to encourage the growth of hazel. An almost invisible horticulture was once practised in the jungles of Guatemala. The spiritual equivalent of Nature-enhancing practices can be seen in those shamanistic disciplines which open the neophyte's mind to that fascinating wild territory, the Unconscious.

We can all agree: there is a problem with the chaotic, self-seeking human ego. Is this a mirror of the wild and of Nature? I think not: for civilization itself is ego gone wild and institutionalized in the form of the State, both Eastern and Western. It is not an imaginary chaos which threatens us (for Nature is orderly) but the sickly entwined *ignorance* of the real, natural world and the mythos of progress, the two together masquerading as 'order'. This sort of 'order' is an elaborate rationalization of the greed and exploitation of a few. Intoxicated by this masquerade, we may blow up the world.

Now we can look again at what sacred land might be. To recapitulate: for a people of an old culture, all their mutually-owned territory holds numinous life and spirits. Certain spots are of high spiritual density because of their perceived animal or plant habitat peculiarities, or associations with legend and perhaps with human ancestry via totemic systems, or because of their geomorphological anomaly and formal intensity, or because of their association with spiritual training, or some combination of the above. These spots are seen as points on the landscape at which one can more easily enter a larger-than-human, larger-than-personal realm.

Nowadays, some present-day inhabitants of Turtle Island, and many Europeans, join with the native peoples of the world in a rather new political and economic movement concerned with 'the ecology'. Stephen Fox says it is also probably a new religion, so new that it has not even been called such yet. Its temples are the planet's remaining wilderness areas. As habitat goes, they are not good. When we enter them on foot we can sense that the *kami* or (Maidu) *kukini* have fled here for refuge, as have the mountain lions, mountain sheep and grizzlies. (Those three North American animals were found throughout the lower hills and plains in pre-White times.) The rocky, icy grandeur of the high country reminds us of the over-arching wild systems that nourish us all – and in the sterile beauty of mountain snowfields and glaciers begin the little streams that water the huge agribusiness fields of the San Joaquin Valley of California. The backpacker-pilgrim's step-by-step, breath-by-breath walk up a trail, carrying all on the back, is so ancient a set of gestures as to trigger perennial images and a profound sense of body-mind joy. 'Sacred' refers to that which takes us out of our little selves into the larger self of the whole universe.

The religious life does not end, however, when one steps outside the doors of the church. The wilderness as a temple is only a first step. That is: one should not dwell in the specialness of the extraordinary experience, not leave the political world behind, to be in a state of heightened insight. The best purpose of such studies and backpack hikes is to be able to come back into the present world to see all the land about us, agricultural, suburban, urban, as part of the same giant realm of processes and beings – never totally ruined, never completely unnatural. Great Brown Bear is walking with us, salmon swimming upstream with us, as we stroll a city street. Every day's a good day – as the Chinese say – and all land's good land.

So, to return to my own situation, the land my family

and I live on 'in the Sierra Nevada of California is 'barely good' from an economic standpoint. With soil amendments, much labour, and the development of ponds for watering, it is producing a few vegetables and some good apples. As forest soils go, it's better: through the millennia it has excelled at growing oak and pine trees. I guess I should admit that it's better left wild. It's being 'managed for wild' right now – the pines are getting large again and some of the oaks were growing here before a white man set foot anywhere in California. The deer and all the other animals move through, with the exception of grizzly bear. Grizzlies are now extinct in California. We dream sometimes of trying to bring them back.

This place is not striking in any special way, with no great scenery or rocks – but the deer are so at home here, I think it might be a 'deer field'. And the fact that I and my neighbours and all of our children have learned so much by taking our place in the lower Sierra foothills – not lovely wilderness, but logged-over land, burned-over land, considered worthless for decades – begins to make it sacred for us. Sacred as a teacher, a place on earth we work with, struggle with, where we stick out the summers and winters. And, moreover, having once known one place well, wherever one travels one can be at home, looking for the signs of health or ailment in forest or soils, noting the style of hoe or axe, sharing tools and information with hill-farmers of Nepal (as I once did) or keepers of little gardens in the city. Only a person who has lived and learned a place through seasons of observation and work, who knows what roots mean, can have an eye to see what's happening with farms or forests around the planet – even when it's strange and out of his home territory. With such knowledge and love we'll fight for a place, too. As Peter Nabokov says, good-hearted urban environmentalists can turn their back on a save-the-wilderness project when it gets too tiresome, and return to a safe home. But inhabitory people will 'fight for their lives like they've been jumped in an alley' – and rightly so.

This small, blue-green planet is the only one with comfortable temperatures, good air and water, a wealth of animals and plants, for millions (or quadrillions) of miles: a little waterhole in the Vast Space, a nesting place, a place of singing and practice, a place of dreaming. It's on the verge of being totally trashed – there's a slow way and a fast way. We are all natives here, and this is our only sacred spot. We must know that we've been jumped, and fight like a racoon in a pack of hounds, for our own and all other lives.

VIII

Life on Earth

Petra Kelly

We can best help you prevent war, not by repeating
your words and repeating your methods, but by finding new words and creating new methods.

Virginia Woolf

On 3 November 1983, I read in the German newspapers with great shock about the warnings of the
British Defence Minister, Michael Heseltine, in which
he made clear that the military police would shoot at
peaceful demonstrators near the American base at
Greenham Common. His warnings led to very strong
reactions on the part of the Opposition and the peace
movement. For it is now clear, very clear, that the laws
in the Western democracies protect the bombs and not
the people! The warning to shoot, the warning that the
state is ready to kill those engaged and committed to
non-violent resistance against mass-destructive
weapons, show how criminal and contrary to international law this atomic age has become and in fact is.

Great Britain, I am told, has more nuclear bases and
consequently more targets per head of population and
per square mile than any country in the world. And I
come from a country, the Federal Republic of Germany, that is armed to the teeth with atomic and conventional weapons. I am here this weekend to give the
E. F. Schumacher Memorial Lecture, and at the same
time to dedicate this lecture to the Greenham Common

women. I dedicate to them a poem by Joan Cavanagh,
which goes as follows:

I am a dangerous woman
Carrying neither bombs nor babies
Flowers nor Molotov cocktails.
I confound all your reason, theory, realism
Because I will neither lie in your ditches
Nor dig your ditches for you
Nor join in your armed struggle
For bigger and better ditches
I will not walk with you nor walk for you.
I won't live with you
And I won't die for you
But neither will I try to deny you
The right to live and die.
I will not share one square foot of this earth with
    you
While you are hell-bent on destruction,
But neither will I deny that we are of the same
    earth,
Born of the same mother.
I will not permit
You to bind my life to yours
But I will tell you that our lives
Are bound together
And I will demand
That you live as though you understand
This one salient fact.

I am a dangerous woman
Because I will tell you, Sir,
Whether you are concerned or not
Masculinity has made of this world a living hell,
A furnace burning away at hope, love, faith and
    justice

A furnace of My-Lais, Hiroshimas, Dachaus.
A furnace which burns the babies
You tell us we must make.
Masculinity made femininity,
Made the eyes of our women go dark and cold
Sent our sons – yes Sir, our sons –
To war
Made our children go hungry
Made our mothers whores
Made our bombs, our bullets, our 'Food for Peace',
    our definitive solutions and first-strike policies.
Masculinity broke women and men on its knee,
Took away our futures,
Made our hopes, fears, thoughts and good instincts
'Irrelevant to the larger struggle'
And made human survival beyond the year 2000
An open question.

I am a dangerous woman
Because I will say all this
Lying neither to you nor with you
Neither trusting nor despising you.
I am dangerous because
I won't give up or shut up
Or put up with your version of reality.
You have conspired to sell my life quite cheaply
And I am especially dangerous
Because I will never forgive nor forget
Or ever conspire
To sell your life in return.

I dedicate these lines to the women at Greenham
Common, who are looking at this planet Earth as their
home, as my home, and themselves as part of everything here. Women all over the world are taking the
lead in defending non-violently the forces of life, the

forests of the Himalayas, demanding a nuclear-free constitution in the Pacific islands called Belau, campaigning against the chemical industry after Seveso, developing a new awareness of the rights of animals and plants and children and unborn children who have no lobby, and demonstrating for peace.

We must show that we have the power to change and that we can contribute towards the development of an ecological/feminist theory, capable of challenging the threat to life before it is too late.

Just a few days ago the American House of Representatives agreed to go ahead with construction of the first twenty-one of one hundred planned MX intercontinental missiles. I have just returned from a trip to the men at the Kremlin in Moscow and to those men in power in East Germany. And I have also been this year several times to Washington to meet those in power there. And during each trip, whether it was to Moscow or Washington or East Berlin, I tried at the same time to speak to and meet the people at the grassroots level – those struggling against the military-industrial complex, whether in its capitalistic or state socialist form. And while I sat listening to those men, those many incompetent men in power, I realized that they are all mirror images of each other. Each threatens the other side and tries to explain that they are forced to do so; that they are forced to plan more evil things to prevent other evil things happening. And that is the heart of the so-called theory of 'atomic deterrence'; that is the heart of the so-called balance of terror, where one side plans more horrifying things in order to outdo the other side.

Today our planetary environment is threatened on a scale unprecedented in human history – from the extinction of species and of laws of genetic diversity, the build-up of toxic and radioactive waste, deforestation and desertification, to the massive alteration in the global climate. And we are watching cowboy economics and cowboy threats; we are watching an industrial order with its competitive, expansionist, machismo, militaristic and patriarchial nation states. Confronting the system of machismo is a trend towards new-age politics, a trend towards eco-feminism. We try to make others aware of basic principles, such as the value of all human beings, the right of all human beings to satisfaction of basic human needs, equality of opportunity for self-development for all human beings, and recognition that these principles and goals must be achieved within ecological tolerances of the land, sea, air, forest, and the total carrying capacity of the biosphere. And the recognition that all these principles apply with equal emphasis to future generations of humans and their biospheric life-support systems, and thus include respect for all other life-forms and the Earth itself.

Susan Griffin wrote, in her foreword of the book *Reclaim the Earth*, that if there is one idea that can be said to link together all that is said and reported, this idea is also a feeling: 'It is a grief over the fate of the Earth, that contains within it a joyful hope that we might reclaim this Earth.' For what we have in common, in this worldwide ecological, feminist and peace movement, is not small. In many countries all over the world, women especially are taking an increasingly prominent role in political struggles, in peace and anti-nuclear and ecological movements. For a growing number of women, this women's-ecological movement has brought about a gradual release from the constraints of traditional women's roles, thus enabling us to reclaim invaluable time and energy. Leonie Caldecott and Stephanie Leland have written: 'This is a slow process, and by no means a universal one as yet. However, within this process, we are gaining a sense of our strength and worth as individuals and, in a collective sense, as women.'

We must realize that the nuclear arms race is in large part underwritten by masculine behaviour in pursuit of the application of scientific enquiry. Modern science is basically a masculine endeavour, and in a world of competing nation states and military blocs it serves to fuel the fires of human conflict rather than to quench them. Masculine science and masculine thinking have already been applied, whether it be in the concentration camps of Auschwitz, in Dresden, in Nagasaki, in Vietnam, in Grenada, in Afghanistan, or in Prague in 1968. But today we are asking many questions such as: why does the arms race continue, and why do military/ industrial/scientific complexes have an insatiable demand for new weapons systems? The arms race, I believe, is insane, but it is an inevitable outcome of science performed in a world where men wage war against feminine values, women and female nature. We must trace the myths and metaphors associated with the so-called conquest of Nature, concluding that humanity's long-term future depends on a radical reevaluation of masculine institutions and ideologies. And those women in power, such as Margaret Thatcher or Indira Gandhi, have only come to power in this male-oriented world because they have adapted themselves to male values and to male ideologies.

The Women's Pentagon Action of November 1980, when many women surrounded the Pentagon for two days of non-violent direct action against all military violence and against sexual and economic violence in the everyday lives of all women, adopted a statement of unity expressing the diverse political concerns of the eco-feminist movement:

We are gathering at the Pentagon because we fear for our lives. We fear for the life of this planet, our Earth, and the life of our children who are our future . . . We have come here to mourn and rage and defy the Pentagon, because it is the workplace of the imperial power which threatens us all. Every day while we work, study, love, the colonels and generals who are planning our annihilation walk calmly in and out the doors of its five sides. They have accumulated over 30,000 nuclear bombs, at the rate of three to six bombs every day . . . They are determined to produce the billion-dollar MX missile. They are creating a technology called Stealth – the invisible unperceivable arsenal. They have revised the cruel old killer, nerve gas. They have proclaimed Directive 59 which asks for small nuclear wars "prolonged" but limited. The Soviet Union works hard to keep up with United States initiatives. We can destroy each other's cities, towns, schools and children many times over . . .

The very same men, the same legislative committees that offered trillions of dollars to the Pentagon, have brutally cut day-care, children's lunches, battered-women's shelters . . . We are in the hands of men whose power and wealth have separated them from the reality of daily life and from the imagination. We are right to be afraid.

We women are gathering because life on the precipice is intolerable. We want to know what anger in these men, what fear which can only be satisfied by destruction, what coldness of heart and ambition drives their days. *We want to know, because we do not want that dominance which is exploitative and murderous in international relations, and so dangerous to women and children at home – we do not want that sickness transferred by the violent society through the fathers to the sons.*

We want to end the arms race. No more bombs, nor more amazing inventions for death. We understand all the connectedness. We know the life and work of animals and plants in feeding, refeeding, and in fact simply inhabiting this planet. Their exploitation and the organized destruction of never-to-be-seen-again species threatens and sorrows us. The Earth nourishes us, as we with our bodies will eventually feed it. Through us our mothers connected the human past to the human future. With that sense, that ecological right, we oppose the financial connections between the Pentagon and the multinational corporations and banks that the Pentagon serves. Those connections are made of gold and oil. We are made of blood and bone, we are made of the sweet and finite resource, water. We will not allow these violent games to continue. *If we are here in our stubborn thousands today, we will certainly return in the hundreds of thousands in the months and years to come.*

(Women's Pentagon Action Unity Statement)

And so, together with my sisters in Greenham Common, we ask for an end to the arms race and an end to interventionist policies in the Third World. As women who have learned to care for Life and to ease conflicts, we know that violence solves nothing. It merely removes parties to conflict which only can be solved without violence. We know that everything is connected. Violence, oppression and domination are all related . . . they are all ways to keep the powerless in their place. The same racism that fuels United States war-making in El Salvador and in Grenada makes it impossible for Blacks and Indians to find jobs or get decent schooling here and elsewhere. The same respect for machismo that breeds wars also encourages rape, pornography and the battering of women. There can

166

be no peace while one race dominates another, or one people, one nation, one sex despises another.

In an American newspaper, the *Times Herald* of 22 September 1983, an 11-year-old girl is cited, telling a House Committee: 'I think instead of worrying so much about nuclear war, we should do something about it. But I'm still scared.' Jessica Fiedler of Iowa was one of three children who together with several experts on child development, testified before the Select Committee on Children, Youth and Families. 'I think about the Bomb just about every day now. It makes me sad and depressed', said another student.

In the typical, helpless male way, one of the members of the House explained that this Committee Hearing on Children's Fears of Nuclear War was being held in order to better understand the behaviour and the hopes and aspirations of children. Several Republican committee members objected to the hearing. 'Defense policy is not a proper subject for this committee, even if their policy is articulated by children', stated one of the members. But what is so frightening is the fact that surveys have been taken in which 80 per cent of the students polled said they thought there would be a nuclear war in the next 20 years. And 81 per cent said that the threat of nuclear war affected their hopes for the future.

In reading recently the summary of the Office of Technology *Assessment on the Effects of Nuclear War*, I came across the most absurd facts and opinions, such as that the times/seasons of the year have a direct effect on the rate of population death during nuclear war. The 'competent' men in power explain that an attack in the dead of winter might not directly damage agriculture but may lead to greater death from fall-out radiation and from cold and exposure. The study becomes even more absurd when it explains that we have not yet found a solution to how to control fires during nuclear wars, because the blast will destroy all fire stations – as actually happened at Hiroshima. Those same high men in high places of power explain that there is no reliable way to estimate the likelihood of such effects. In fact, they openly question the physical and psychological vulnerability of a population during a nuclear attack. The study states: 'Even more critical would be the events after the attack', then goes on further to state: 'Assuming that war ends promptly, the terms on which it ends could greatly affect both the economic condition and state of mind of the population.' And if you seek yet more irony and more perversion, then please read the study's conclusion: 'The post-attack military situation could not only determine the attitude of other countries, but also whether limited surviving resources are put to military or to civilian use.' As you see, those men in places of power are worrying about whether or not the remaining survivors are put to military or to civilian use. So the children of the world have a right to speak about their fears of a nuclear-era life.

Philip Berrigan, a dear friend of mine and a friend of the Green Party, has made the following comment:

We are moving in the direction of mass suicide and total annihilation, all in the name of so-called legality. There are governments who are continuously breaking the law at national and international level. These governments behave in an illegal and uncontrolled manner. Without the cloak of legality, these governments could not carry out this atomic insanity. And for that reason, we must call our actions 'non-violent civil disobedience' even though they are in reality civil obedience.

We, the Green Party, are not only indicting the

Federal Government but also *all* the governments of *all* nuclear powers, whether it be the United States, the Soviet Union, Great Britain, France, China or India, as well as all states which are secretly acquiring atomic weapons through the civilian nuclear fuel cycle. We indict the nuclear powers because their willingness to use atomic weapons removes the very foundations of international law and of human rights; because their threat to use such weapons infringes the general rules of international law; because they have not observed their accepted obligations to achieve nuclear disarmament; because advances in weapons technology, without any political controls, make an atomic war inevitable, and thus nullify the fundamental right enjoyed by all living and future human beings to existence and security.

By virtue of the decisions taken by the NATO foreign affairs and defence ministers on 12 December 1979, namely to deploy new medium-range American missiles suitable for offensive and first-strike warfare in Western Europe, and in particular on the territory of my country, the Federal Republic of Germany, NATO has manifestly and explicitly quit the phase of being a defensive alliance, and has assumed the character of a military alliance with offensive intentions which thus also risk a war of aggression. We know that the Greenham Common women have gone to court in the United States. The Green Party also in 1981 launched criminal charges against Helmut Schmidt and Hans-Dietrich Genscher for their betrayal of peace and specifically for 'preparing a war of aggression'. The German Penal Code states, with reference to the betrayal of peace:

Anyone who prepares a war of aggression in which the Federal Republic of Germany is to take part, and thus precipitates the danger of a war for the Federal Republic of Germany, is liable to a punishment of life-long imprisonment or a term of imprisonment of not less than 10 years.

In February of this year (1983) in Nuremberg, the Green Party held, through my own initiation and contribution, a War Crimes Tribunal against First Strike and Mass-Destructive Weapons in East and West. We made it quite clear during that tribunal that we, the people, must put on trial the political and military leaders who are dragging heaven into hell.

We must reverse the trend if there is to be any security. Today the arsenals of the atomic powers have the explosive power of well over one million Hiroshima bombs. Nuclear superiority is completely meaningless when so many thousands of weapons are already in existence. The so-called balance of terror is also meaningless, when each side can kill the other ten or twelve times over.

The United States now has 9,500 strategic nuclear weapons, and the USSR has about 7,700. This is a so-called perverse rough equality between their strategic arsenals. No defence against these weapons exists. Neither side, now or in the foreseeable future can disarm the other in a successful first strike. Thus first-strike weapons such as Pershing II, which can 'decapitate' the other side, are now to be deployed, creating a second Cuban Crisis in Europe!

At present, NATO doctrine includes the first use of tactical nuclear weapons to repel a non-nuclear attack. The use of such weapons on the battlefield can swiftly escalate to all-out nuclear war, which would devastate much of the northern hemisphere. The NATO Alliance has the manpower, economic wealth and technological prowess to mount an adequate conventional defence against a non-nuclear attack by the Soviet Union. This is stated even by US General Kroesen, who has stated that NATO need *not* resort to any nuclear weapons in the event of a so-called non-nuclear attack. Nuclear war is most likely to begin as an outgrowth of conventional war, through miscalculation, through errors in computers, or as an act of desperation. The advent of new nuclear weapons that are more threatening and more accurate heightens the risk of an attempted preemptive attack. Most of the new nuclear weapons are less easy to verify, thus making arms control treaties even more difficult to achieve. We have asked for so long that NATO should announce its intention of adopting a policy of 'no first use' of nuclear weapons in Europe. The United States also should announce its intention of adopting a policy of 'no first use' of nuclear weapons elsewhere in the world. And we feel that all nuclear powers, including France and Great Britain, must immediately sit down at the negotiating table, placing all sea-, air- and land-based systems on that negotiating table, and start honestly to reduce their arsenals.

The so-called 'zero' (and also partial) option and solution as put forth by Ronald Reagan is a completely hypocritical one, for it ignores, in dealing with reductions of arms, all those existing NATO weapons on our side. It asks for the removal and scrapping of SS-20s, SS-4s and SS-5s, but, in fact, NATO, during the talks in Geneva, does not agree to reduce any existing nuclear weapon on our side except for some of the old ones that they are about to replace. We have demanded that the British and French potentials be counted, for even in the 1979 White Book of our Defence Ministry they were counted as part of the NATO package. Many of you know that the senior NATO commander has powers of decision-making as regards use of those potentials in Europe. The Congressional Study of the Library of Congress of the United States has also demanded that the British and French nuclear forces be counted in the INF negotiations, and thus Mr Andropov's proposals are ones which could lead us out of the nuclear dilemma now created in Geneva.

We are asking, as we have asked in Moscow, that Mr Andropov and the men in the Kremlin go far beyond those proposals: that is to say, they should initiate unilaterally their proposals whether or not there is a successful outcome in Geneva. We have asked that the Soviet Union begin dismantling their SS-20s down to the so-called 'balance of terror' which they admitted to existing in 1979. They should start unilaterally to scrap and dismantle SS-20s while the talks in Geneva are still being held up to 17 November. We feel that this will not be a threat to their so-called military security, for they will still be in possession of many other types of nuclear weapons, and need not feel 'insecure' when unilaterally dismantling one system.

We in Western Europe that are part of the European peace movement are doing everything possible this autumn and winter to stop the deployment of the American missiles, through civil disobedience and active non-violence. We are drawing distinctions between what is legal and legitimate, and we maintain that certain illegal non-violent acts may be legitimate as a last resort against morally wrong decisions made by our governments. We realize that legal rights and moral rights are not always identical. *At this time we feel that we have a citizen's duty to disobey*! We feel that non-violent civil resistance to the deployment of the NATO missiles is morally correct, because these weapons create an irreversible new situation which is leading us to war and is reducing the chances of survival of future generations. We realize that by engaging in civil disobedience we are breaking the law and must therefore take punishment into account. Non-violent action is for us a means to combat existing or threatening forms of violence. Non-violent action attempts to provide an answer not only to the question, 'What do we do if the Russians come?' but also to the increasingly urgent question, 'What do we do if the Americans stay, and against our will deploy in our countries new weapons of mass extermination?' We are against *all* foreign troops in the countries of the world, and thus we also ask the Soviet Union to leave Afghanistan and the Americans to leave Grenada.

Non-violent measures are aimed at achieving disarmament, at detecting, removing and counteracting the existing forms of violence. The opponent is given an opportunity to reconsider, to change his behaviour and to recognize that it is his role as agent of the power of the state that is under attack, and not himself as an individual. Henry David Thoreau stated:

> If, however, the law is so promulgated that it of necessity makes you an agent of injustice against another, then I say to you – break the law.

We must find a way to 'demilitarize' society if we are to succeed. And so we must deny votes to the exponents of rearmament and weapons of mass destruction. We must refuse military conscription and resist the call of military service for women. We must organize alternative production in the arms industry and move toward the production of socially useful goods, and we must organize political strikes and war-tax boycotts in order to make clear that we are no longer part of this system of violence. We want to change the structures and conditions of our society non-violently and move towards a system of social, alternative defence. We declare ourselves responsible for security policies

within our own immediate surroundings. We are becoming experts over our own lives.

At a time when one quarter of all the world's nations
are currently involved in wars; when 45 of the world's
164 nations are involved in 40 conventional and guerilla
conflicts; when over 4 million soldiers this very day are
directly engaged in combat; when about 500,000 foreign combat troops are involved in 8 conflicts; when
the United States, Great Britain, Germany, France and
the Soviet Union are major arms suppliers to about 40
of these nations at war; I would like to leave you with
these words:

> O sisters, come you sing for all you're worth
> Arms are made for linking.
> Sisters, we're asking for the Earth.

Gandhi stated that non-violence is the greatest force
man has ever been endowed with. And love has more
force and power than a besieging army. The force of
this power of love, as Martin Luther King said, is
'passive physically, but strongly active spiritually' – that
is, 'while the non-violent resister is passive in the sense
that he is not physically aggressive toward his opponent, his mind and his emotions are constantly active,
constantly seeking to persuade the opposition.'

These spiritual weapons do what guns and arms only
pretend to do – they defend us. These spiritual weapons
can bring about, I believe, the kind of great social
change and the kind of social force that we need in this
destructive age.

IX

Split Culture

Susan Griffin

We who are born into this civilization have inherited a habit of mind. We are divided against ourselves. We no longer feel ourselves to be a part of this earth. We regard our fellow creatures as enemies. And, very young, we even learn to disown a part of our own being. We come to believe that we do not know what we know. We grow used to ignoring the evidence of our own experience, what we hear or see, what we feel in our own bodies. We come into maturity keeping secrets. But we forget this secret knowledge and feel instead only a vague shame, a sense that perhaps we are not who we say we are. Yet we have learned well to pretend that what is true is not true. In some places the sky is perpetually grey, and the air filled with a putrid smell. Forests we loved as children disappear. The waters we once swam are forbidden to us now because they are poisoned. We remember there was a sweet taste to fruit, that there used to be more birds. But we do not read these perceptions as signs of our own peril. Long ago we gave up ourselves. Now, if we are dying by increments, we have ceased to be aware of this death. How can we know our own death if we do not know our own existence? We have traded our real existence, our real feelings for a delusion. Instead of fighting for our lives, we bend all our efforts to defend delusion. We deny all evidence at hand that this civilization which has shaped our minds is also destroying the earth.

The dividedness of our minds is etched into our language. To us, the word 'thought' means an activity separate from feeling, just as the word 'mind' suggests a place apart from the body and from the rhythms of the earth. We do not use the word 'animal' to describe human qualities. Our word 'spirit' rises in our imaginations above the earth as if we believed that holiness exists in an inverse proportion to gravity. The circumstance of our birth is common to us; we are all of woman born. But we have a word 'race' which suggests to us that human beings belong to different categories of virtue by birth. Through the words 'masculine' and 'feminine', which we use to designate two alien and alienated poles of human behaviour, we make our sexuality a source of separation. We divide ourselves and all that we know along an invisible borderline between what we call 'Nature' and what we believe is superior to Nature.

Now we find ourselves moving almost without recourse towards a war that will destroy all of our lives. And were this not true, we have learned that the way we live has damaged the atmosphere, our bodies, even our genetic heritage so severely that perhaps we cannot save ourselves. We are at the edge of death, and yet, like one who contemplates suicide, we are our own enemies. We think with the very mind that has brought disaster on us. And this mind, taught and trained by this civilization, does not know itself. This is a mind in exile from its own wisdom.

This is a mind which defines itself as exclusively masculine. If this mind denies that it is part of Nature, it asserts that the feminine mind is closer to Nature. But it does not see this proximity as a virtue.

When St Augustine wrote that 'not the woman but

the man is the image of God', he was both thinking within and helping to create a paradigm which still shapes our thoughts. Within the same paradigm it has been asserted, for instance by Mallebranche, that because women menstruate regularly the fibres of our brains are weaker, and thus our minds are defective. Or it has been stated, for example by Robert Boyle, that matter 'is but a brute thing and only capable of local motion.' And the same paradigm argues, through the words of René Descartes, that animals cannot have immortal souls since 'there are many of them too imperfect to make it possible to believe it of them, such as oysters, sponges etc.'

According to this world-view, a view whose assumptions are so widely accepted by this civilization that we do not even think of it as an ideology, there is a hierarchy to existence. God and the angels, things pure in spirit and devoid of any material content, come first. Everything earthly is corrupt. But among the corrupt, human beings are of the highest spiritual order, more significant, valuable and trustworthy than animals, or certainly trees or, of course, tomatoes, and obviously more intelligent than mountains, or oceans, or particles of sand. Among human beings a similar order exists. Those of the human species who belong to what is thought of as the white race, and those who are part of the masculine gender, are at the top of this hierarchy. Various glosses on the fundamental belief place the rest of us in different descending orders. Yet among the unfortunate creatures of the earth, white men are described as 'God's Viceroy', appointed to wield dominion over women, children, those of other 'races', animals, plants and the geography.

It is under the influence of this paradigm that in a traditional marriage a man is the head of the household; women take out the garbage – scapegoats even for ecological damage. Because of social beliefs and institutions shaped by this paradigm, few of our mothers are educated, and we do not earn salaries equal to men. This paradigm has shaped human behaviour. It is the fundamental thought behind strip-mining, and the destruction of whole forests. It is the paradigm which underlies rape and pornography. It is a paradigm which has shaped history, giving us not only the scientific and industrial revolutions but also the Inquisition, the witchburnings and the Holocaust.

We have learned of the scientific revolution that it was a victory over the irrational, over magical thought, which led to the Inquisition and the witchburnings. And we do not commonly associate the philosophy of St Augustine about men and women with the scientific world-view, because we are accustomed to thinking that science and religion are at opposite positions in that polemic which expressed itself in the trial of Galileo. Despite the fact that Galileo recanted to the Church, we no longer believe the world was literally created in seven days, nor do we place the earth at the centre of the Solar System.

But what we have not considered is that a civilization may suffer a great transformation in its institutions and its philosophy – power can shift from Church to State, and the authority for knowledge from priest to scientist – and yet still retain, in a new guise and a new language, the essence of the old point of view. Such is the case with the scientific revolution, so that many assumptions, methods and even questions which we take to be scientific actually partake of the same paradigm which in an earlier age we described as Christian.

Let us look at Newton's *Optics* for an example. Before Newton's work on optics, many different ideas about vision were believed, including the notion that a ray of light emanated from the human eye and illuminated the world. Through observation and experiment, Newton concluded that colour is not a property of the eye nor the property of any object but is instead produced by the retina, sensitive to light refracted at different angles. This and like discoveries in the 17th and 18th century fell into a philosophical doctrine which was taken to be an experimentally proven vision of the true nature of the world. The scientific point of view argued that we cannot trust our senses, that we are deceived by the appearance of the material world, that colour is a form of illusion; that colour is simply a figment of our minds, and does not exist.

Thus if religion told us that the earth was a corrupt place, that our true home was heaven, that sensual feeling was not to be trusted and could lead us to hell and damnation, science did not in essence contradict that doctrine. For science too told us not to trust our senses, that matter is deceptive and that we are alien to our surroundings. If then religion told us that our own senses could not be trusted and that therefore we must bow to Scripture and the authority of the priest, now science tells us that we must bow to the truth of objective experimental data, and the authority of scientific experts. In both systems, not only are we alienated from a world which is described as deceiving us; we are also alienated from our own capacity to see and hear, to taste and touch, to know and describe our own experience.

Such is the strength of this old way of thinking – that the earth and what is natural in ourselves is not to be trusted – that it hardly occurs to us there is another way to interpret Newton's discovery; we have confused his discovery with our old paradigmatic vision.

For indeed one can make a very different interpretation of Newton's observations of the nature of optics. Instead of believing that we are deceived by matter or our senses, insteading of deciding that colour does not exist, we can assert, since we do experience colour, that in our experience of colour we have entered into a union with what we perceive. That together with matter we create colour. That our sense of colour is indeed evidence of a profound, sensual and emotional connection which we have with all that is part of this earth. That the joy which colour gives us is perhaps part of the balance of the universe.

There is another example of how the old paradigm affects what we take to be impartial science, from Francis Bacon's argument that science ought to proceed by experimentation. It must be close to self-evident, one can object here, that scientific experimentation is a movement towards respect of the material world. Before the idea of experiment, the nature of the material world was not even considered worthy of observation. Speculation and deductive reason were the sources of truth. I must digress for a moment with this to point out that if one is part of Nature oneself, speculation, especially when it involves self-reflection, *is* a kind of experiment. And perhaps this is not really a digression. For indeed, what is missing in Bacon's idea of scientific experiment is any self-reflection. He assumes that a superior objectivity, a state of emotional and physical detachment, can belong to the scientist who performs an experiment.

Let us for a moment forget Heisenberg's principle of uncertainty and pretend that we do not know from experiment what Bacon, indeed, did not know either: that the observer always changes what is observed through the act of observation. Let us look only at Bacon's language, the language he uses to describe the scientific method, for it is not a detached luggage. It is full of emotion. He suggests, for example, that 'Nature must be hounded in her wanderings before one can lead her and drive her.' This is hardly an objective relationship to the material world. It is one, I might add, with which women are familiar. We are used to being scrutinized as if we were prey to be hunted. And this comparison is not casual, for Bacon also writes, again using the feminine pronoun to represent Nature, that 'the earth should be put on the rack and tortured for her secrets.' So that now the object of experimentation is not the animal who is hunted but the witch who is interrogated, tortured and burned.

Since most of us have been taught that the spirit of scientific inquiry lead to the eventual end of the witch-burnings, one is surprised to discover that the period of greatest scientific discovery, the years of the scientific revolution, from the 14th through the 18th century, were also the years of the greatest numbers of witch-burnings. Far from the acts of ignorant men, the witch-burners were the most educated men of their day. In fact, many scientists, including William Harvey, assisted at the examination of witches, and rendered scientific judgements concerning who was and who was not a witch.

That Bacon used the torturing of a witch as a metaphor for the scientific examination of matter is not an accident. This metaphor reveals to us the inner workings of his mind. He had the church's attitude towards Nature. He was not a detached observer. He felt that he was interrogating an enemy. He recommended cruelty towards that enemy; one might even say that for him the pursuit of knowledge was an expression of fear and rage.

In different ages, both religion and science have been the focus of our hopes and the arbiters of what we call truth. Because they have expressed the consciousness of a whole civilization, both institutions also carry with them and, in their ideas and traditions, epitomize the troubled conflict, the dividedness of our consciousness. Both institutions within Western civilization have been shaped by and have deepened our alienation from this earth.

If the Church once offered the denigration of incarnate life as a solution to the human condition, now science offers us the control of matter as our rescue. But what can be wrong with cultivating either the human spirit or the soil we live on? Human creativity is a part of Nature, but rather we think of ourselves as working against Nature. The paradigm which tells us that we are apart from and above this earth is not simply an intellectual response to Nature. It is instead a deeply fearful attitude. And the fear which lies under this thought, like all fear, turns into rage. A rage that is as dangerous to us now as the Church fires were dangerous to the lives of women and men burned as witches.

The pursuit of scientific knowledge in our civilization is beset by an emotional dilemma. In order to control Nature, we must know Nature. But just as we are seeking to know, there is a knowledge we fear. We are afraid to remember what we, in our bodies, in our feelings, still know, but what, in our fragmented, civilized consciousness we have been persuaded to forget. That, like the forests we destroy, or the rivers we try to tame, *we* are Nature.

The discovery of the Solar System, of gravitational law, of evolution, of the microscopic world of the cell, of the genetic information which is part of matter, of the nature of light, and of the continuum between matter and energy, should transform consciousness so that we in this civilization might begin to regard the human condition with humility rather than arrogance. The thinkers who made what we call the scientific revolution had begun to discover a vast matrix of natural order, a very large wisdom whose boundaries we cannot even imagine. Just as the Earth is not the centre of the Solar System, so the biosphere is not centred on the human species, nor circumscribed by human culture. We are dependent on the universe around us not only to breathe, to eat, but even to keep our feet on the ground. For we do this not at will but because we exist in a field of energy. All that we do is shaped by and partakes of that field. And our perceptions and what we experience as real depend upon the nature and the movements of matter and light. Not only are we mortal, but the very human form suffers a slow change over generations. Between my arm and the air, between the movements of a flame and what we call the solid mass of wood, there is no boundary.

But we have come to rely upon another image of ourselves: as discrete static beings. And we have learned to think that we must take control of our environment in order to survive. We believe that it is a cultural order, the order we have willed, and not natural order, the order of which we are a part, that makes us safe. Thus, if the discoveries of modern science have given us the means to manipulate Nature, they have also terrified us. And this is why in the fourteenth century, when science began to challenge our old idea of who we are, the witchburnings began. The slave trade began in the 16th century at the height of this revolution in thought. And in the twentieth century, when science again questioned the old notion that we are above nature, the Nazi Holocaust and now the nuclear holocaust have commenced.

Before the Holocaust the Fascist theorist Bruno Thuring described Einstein's ideas as a Jewish plot to 'relativize all concepts'. He complained that this must lead to 'chaos'. The Nazi ideologist Alfred Rosenberg used the term 'the Albert Einsteins' to refer to Jewish intellectuals and artists. And it is true that their scientists and scientific thinkers were persecuted during the Inquisition. But in fact, as we have seen, with Newton and Bacon, the surprising new concepts of science were successfully moulded into the old paradigm of the Church that the human is above Nature. And if the Third Reich rejected the philosophical implications of relativity, it put the new physics to use in an effort to build nuclear weapons. We now know that it was in competition with Germany's efforts that American scientists finally succeeded in building the first atom bombs. Rather than transform consciousness, scientific knowledge has been used by our civilization to fortify the illusion that we control Nature.

Yet whatever we attempt to exile from awareness come back to haunt us. If we attempt to divide ourselves from what we know, the mind invents a figment of this denied knowledge which returns to trouble us. Here is the meeting place between social oppression and the destruction of the environment by human society. For racism, anti-semitism and the oppression of women all serve to hide from civilization what it knows yet does not wish to know. The Jew or the Black or the woman become at one and the same time a symbol of Nature and a symbol of the denied natural self: this self which, in the body, experiences Nature, through sensation, emotion, the memory of birth, the anticipation of danger, or loss, through grief, love and anger. When the witchburners Kramer and Sprenger stated that women have 'inordinate affections and passions', or when Martin Luther wrote that woman 'is not fully the master of herself', these men were not describing real women but a part of the human psyche which culture teaches us to bury. As the American writer James Baldwin has said, the idea of the 'nigger' describes the mind of the white racist.

When the anti-semite says that he knows the Jew is plotting to seize power, he is speaking the truth about a part of his own mind. The knowledge of his own body cannot be forgotten. He must breathe. He must become hungry, grow tired. He cannot rid himself of the emotions which well up in his body and may cause him to weep, or make his heart race. What he feels attempts over and over to enter his consciousness through his dreams, through shadow thoughts. For like Nature, the human mind is whole. It has an ecology, a natural balance. And it cannot be divided except that it will attempt to return to itself. So the anti-semite imagines that his own mind plots to overpower him. The witchburner imagines the witch at a sexual orgy, or eating human flesh.

But in separating Nature from culture within himself, the man who believes this delusion has split his own needs and desires from his intelligence and from all meaning. Thus his own desires return to him as meaningless, as cruel and senseless violations. Out of the lost fragments of his own psyche, he has created a monstrous image to contain his own self-loathing. Thus the pornographer creates out of his own sexual desires a meeting between two bodies that is without emotion, without any deep or soulful connection. And when he invents a woman, a pornographic heroine, he gives her a body without a spirit, without any sensibility, without a significant consciousness. She is like the dead matter, the brute matter, of scientific theory.

And the modern mind invents the same image of Nature itself. Matter is dead. A forest has no spiritual life. When Reagan was Governor of California, he said in response to ecologists who were trying to preserve the great coastal forests, 'If you have seen one tree you have seen them all.' Believing a mountain to have no inner reason, no sacredness unto itself, the modern technologist takes coal out of the soil simply by cutting away half of the face of the mountain. Suddenly the whole of the mountain begins to erode. Chemicals from this erosion enter the streams in an unnatural balance. Trees plants, fish, animals die. The countryside which was once breathtakingly beautiful begins to look like a place of devastation. He transforms the mountain into what he believed the mountain to be.

In the same way, society transforms those who have become symbols of Nature into objects of degradation. If a woman is a symbol of Nature, wherever she is pictured as submissive, or wherever she is disempowered in the social order, we can believe that culture has a supernatural power over Nature. If the Jew, who we imagine plots against us, is stripped of all civil rights, we can believe that we have control over natural power. Even those of us who suffer materially and psychologically from this delusory system of control have been educated to feel a false sense of safety from it.

Yet indeed none of us are safe. Now our lives are, every one of us, endangered by this delusion. For the delusion itself cannot rest. It is like the hungry tiger of our fearful dreams: devouring.

When the technologist destroys the mountain, he must feel, momentarily, a false sense of triumph. Like the explorers of an earlier age, he has conquered this piece of earth. He has wrested from her what he wanted. He has beaten her. And yet now as he looks on the devastation he has caused, he cannot help but see there an image of his own inner life. His soul has been robbed by this theft. The death he sees before him must at one and the same time remind him of the part of himself that he has murdered and his own inevitable mortality, which, in the very act of controlling Nature, he has tried to deny.

Through pornography a man has succeeded in capturing an image of a woman, nude, diminished and humiliated. But as he looks on this image, though he feels himself to be more powerful than she and more dignified by the social order, her body simply reminds him of his own sexual feeling. As he begins to feel desire, his own feelings overpower him. He is no longer culture ordering Nature. He is defeated.

And the sight of her body takes him back to that moment where he first learned to associate a woman's body with Nature. When he was a child this body fed him. This woman held his life in her hands. It was she who comforted his fears, or who left him to fear her absence. Her body meant warmth to him, sustenance. And also all the sufferings of the human body and the imagination: grief, loss, pain. In memory, the sight of a woman's body takes this man back to a time when he was vulnerable before Nature, and without culture to tell him that he is a master.

The very images and avenues which are meant to express our power over Nature take us back to our own memory and knowledge of Nature's power both inside and outside of ourselves. Therefore our delusion demands that we gain a greater control over Nature. We must escalate our efforts. We must improve our technology.

One can see the dimensions of this madness clearer in the development of the nuclear power industry. At each turning point, when a piece of human technology was seen to fail, the architects of this industry never questioned the fundamental premise that we are meant to make use of the energy inside the atom by splitting matter apart. Instead another technological solution was offered. And each technological solution has in turn posed a greater danger of risk.

Repeatedly one reads in the newspapers that an error

187

in the design of a nuclear power plant has been covered over by the men who build and operate the plants. In many cases the economic motivation for such a denial is clear. To design the plant properly would take many more millions of dollars. But even given this economic motive, one wonders why these men, who often live in the area of the plant and work there every day, are not afraid for their own lives or the lives of their families. But the answer is that they rely for a feeling of safety not on rational information about natural law, but on the delusion that culture, through technology or any other means, can control Nature.

In this same way we can understand the extreme economic irrationality of nuclear power. For nuclear power is extremely expensive, and there is very little reasonable information which would lead us to believe it will ever benefit society economically, even if we did not face the problem of nuclear waste. And yet, to the mind possessed by delusion, nuclear power offers something money cannot buy. For contained within the image of men splitting apart the atom and stealing the energy from inside is the secret hope of immortality.

At its root, the word 'matter' recalls the word 'mother'. To penetrate Nature at her source, to render apart matter, is to go inside the body of the mother and tear out the secret of life. Hence nuclear power which so threatens all of our lives actually represents, to the deluded mind, the hope of a freedom from death.

But once again, the delusion falls, as it always must. For nuclear power creates plutonium waste. Even a microscopic particle can cause cancer. Now we are suffering an epidemic of cancer which many believe is caused by radiation, and other pollution. The deadly substance increases daily. There is no safe place to keep it, no way to contain it. It is unmanageable – and endless. It is as close an image of death itself as has ever been created.

The mind which invents a delusion of power over Nature in order to feel safe is afraid of fear itself. And the more this mind learns to rely on delusion, the less tolerance this mind has for any betrayal of that delusion. For we must remember that this mind has denied that it itself is a thing of Nature. It has begun to identify not only its own survival, but its own existence with culture. The mind believes that it exists because what it thinks is true. Therefore, to contradict delusion is to threaten the mind's very existence. And the ideas, words, numbers, concepts have become more real to this mind than material reality.

Thus when this mind is threatened by a material danger, it does not respond rationally. For this mind has lost touch with material reality. It is a mind possessed by madness, by a hallucinated idea of its own power. We can see such a mind at work in Stalin, during the period of Soviet industrialization. In this period, the Soviet Union as a nation faced the grave material danger of hunger and starvation. And yet, as a solution, Stalin chose to destroy real and operating farms before the new, sanctioned way of farming was functioning. Issac Deutscher writes vividly of this cast of mind, 'The whole experiment seemed to be a piece of prodigious insanity, in which all the rules of logic and principles of economics were turned upside down. It was as if a whole nation had suddenly abandoned and destroyed its houses and huts, which, though obsolete and decaying, existed in reality, and moved, lock stock and barrel, into some illusory buildings.'

But what is essential to understand about this mind is that it is in a panic. It will go to any lengths to defend its delusory idea of reality. Those who opposed Stalin's plans for collectivization were sent to prison camps or murdered. And the extent to which a belief in ideas over reality is a part of this century was predicted by George Orwell in his novel, *1984*, through the humorous but now distressingly accurate parody of a governmental slogan which he invented, 'Peace is War'. Thus today it is actually presented as a rational argument that a build-up in arms, or a 'preventative' invasion of another country, is the best way to keep peace.

We all understand economic motivation as fundamental to human nature. And yet we are making a mistake if we believe that this is the only motivation. For economics touch upon reality. It would, after all, be of no economic profit to anyone living to destroy the earth. Such a destruction could only be seen as profitable by a madman. But it is madness and the motivations of madness which I am describing here today.

It is only when we understand how economic motivation can be shaped and changed by this madness that we can begin to see the real danger that our culture's state of delusion poses for us. Let us take the slave trade for an example. There is an obvious economic profit to be gained by adventurers from the sale of other human beings. And yet we must question whether simple self-interest leads naturally to such a violation of other beings. Is it not a soul already distorted that can consider enslaving another human being?

Self-interest, the desire to survive, is simply part of flesh, an emotion which arises in us by virtue of our material existence, by virtue even of our love for life and for this earth. But early in childhood we are taught that our survival depends on a freedom from natural power. We are taught that we live not through the understanding of Nature but through the manipulation of Nature.

If one studies the definitions of liberty in the *Oxford English Dictionary* one sees that liberty, first defined as an 'exemption or release from captivity, bondage or slavery', later becomes 'the faculty or power to do as one likes', and then becomes 'an unrestrained use of or access to' – as in 'to take liberties with a wench' – and finally, liberty means 'at one's power or disposal'.

Like the Inquisition and the witchburnings, the slave trade began at the time of the scientific revolution, the 16th century. This revolution threatened to change the old world-view that men ordered Nature and replace it with an understanding of a natural law to which we are all subject. The delusion that we are free from natural law was endangered. But that freedom could be regained symbolically by enslaving a people whom this culture conceived as symbols of Nature. At this time and through the 19th century it was both scientific and a general belief that Africans were closer to Nature than white men and women. In the 19th century, after evolutionary theory, scientists argued that Africans has descended more directly from primates.

It is no coincidence that slavery is associated with exploration both historically and in the imagination. The Great White Explorer personifies our civilization's ideal of masculine freedom. This is the man who is tied down by no woman. He is unafraid of death or pain. He conquers whole portions of the Earth, and brings back the heads of wild animals as trophies of his prowess. But these animals' heads repose in the most civilized rooms, for he himself is not wild but the master of the wilderness.

That the slave trade was not motivated by simple economic self-interest becomes most clear when one studies the conditions which had to be endured by the men, women and children taken into captivity on the slave ships. So many died during these trips across the water, not only from disease and exposure to the elements but also from the brutality of the slave-traders. Had these men valued their cargo from a simple economic motive they might have taken more care to preserve these lives. But instead an unwonted measure of cruelty entered their acts. Ruth and Jacob Weldon, an African couple who experienced a slave passage, recorded an incident of a child of nine months who was flogged continuously for refusing to eat. Because this beating failed to move the child to eat, the captain ordered that 'the child be placed feet first into a pot of boiling water. After trying other tortuous methods with no success, the captain dropped the child and caused its death. Not deriving enough satisfaction from this sadistic act, he then commanded the mother to throw the body of the child overboard. The mother refused but she was beaten until she submitted.'

That Bell Hooks called this behaviour 'sadistic' is entirely fitting. Clearly, to murder a child in order to get that child to eat is not rational behaviour. Rather, the motive lay elsewhere, with the desire to inflict cruelty for its own sake. But why is it that a slave-trader should be cruel to a black child? Because of his blackness this child became, in the insane mind of this civilization, and in the mind of this captain, a symbol of natural power. And the infancy of the boy would remind this man of his own infancy, of his own memory of vulnerability, of his own naturalness. Thus, at one and the same time, he could show his power over Nature, and punish his own vulnerable child, the child within him who was still part of Nature. Underneath his hatred and his cruelty existed a profound self-hatred.

Each time that the child refused to do as he ordered, he was, in an undiscovered region of his own soul, terrified. For this could only mean that he was losing his power, and therefore that his whole existence was being threatened. In this way, the captain could believe that he murdered a nine-month-old child in defence of himself. And if a part of him suffered with that child, he could punish his own compassion, and compassion itself, by forcing the child's mother to throw the child overboard. For such a compassion is also dangerous to this mind, since compassion brings us back to our own capacity to feel.

The same blend of economic and symbolic motivation inspired the Holocaust. At the time of Hitler's rise to power, Germany suffered from a terrible economic depression. And at the same time the old paradigmatic view of man at the centre of the universe was again being threatened by scientific discovery. The Nazi Party identified the Jew as responsible for the economic privation. But what is the emotional experience of economic poverty? It is not simply the absence of money that is felt, but the absence of food, or shelter, or safety. Poverty, or even economic insecurity, places us at the mercy of Nature. We become afraid of loss, of suffering, of death. In its delusion of power over Nature, the European mind had made the Jew the symbol of nature. Thus, frightened by economic insecurity and by a changing world-view, the Nazi stripped the Jew of civil rights and of the right to own possessions.

But it was not necessary for the Jewish people to resist this injustice in order for the Third Reich, like the captain of the slave ship, to feel threatened. For Nature has a way of continually breaking through delusion, whether in the form of economics, through the natural environment or through our own bodies.

If the anti-semite believes he has subdued Nature by making it illegal for the Jew to own property, his belief is challenged by an experience which is inside him and all around him, which *is* Nature and therefore cannot be subdued. Perhaps the economy does go the way he predicts and circumstances force certain privations. If the Third Reich briefly restored employment and thus a certain measure of security, the Second World War soon made daily life difficult again. Or the Nazi may succeed in making his own body into a military machine which follows his orders, but his body itself rebels with feelings he did not anticipate, even giving him emotions which do not fit into his scheme of power. Even the sensation of coldness or sleepiness may remind him that he is a material being and not the *Obermensch* of his delusionary madness.

But when nature thus breaks through to his consciousness, he does not change his philosophy. One who is gripped by madness rarely accepts material evidence that he is mad. Moreover, it was part of the Fascist mind to give up perception and replace it with ideological conviction. Hannah Arendt has written of the German people in that time that, for instance, 'instead of deserting the leaders who had lied to them, they would protest that they had known all along the statement was a lie and praise their leaders for their superior tactical cleverness.' So, despite the fact that the Nazi has stripped the Jew of all social, political and economic power, he still blames his own powerlessness to control nature on the Jew. He ascribes to the Jew the almost magical, certainly supernatural, powers to which he himself aspires, as if his enemy had stolen these powers from him. And indeed such is the case, for he has projected his own nature onto the Jew, and now his idea of the Jew possesses what is his. In the idea of the Jew is his own connectedness with Nature and the deeper wisdom which is part of Nature. Thus his relationship to the Jew must always be a love-hate affair. He may begin by exiling the Jew. But soon the Third Reich annexes those countries to which the Jewish people were exiled. The mind afraid of Nature still cannot simply make Nature vanish from consciousness. So the hunter displays the heads of animals that he has shot in his rooms. And a civilization at war with what it calls 'bestial' adorns itself with leather and fur and feathers, and uses plaster casts of animals to decorate the landscape. The racist keeps a small figure of Aunt Jemima or a stable boy, and in this way he can both have and not have the part of himself he denies. Claiming that he cannot bear the presence of women, the member of an exclusive men's club stirs his drink with a swizzle stick fashioned after a woman's body. In America, at the exclusive Bohemian Club to which the most powerful men have belonged, the male membership frequently dress up as women in order to put on plays. Yet, even if the deluded mind is able to recapture itself in a diminished, humiliated form, still it is at war with and terrified by the self.

Thus Hitler orders the Jewish people into concentration camps. But he is not content to imprison his enemy. Once there he must torture them. As Otto Fenichel has written, contained within anti-semitism is the cruel suppression and punishment of instinctual rebellion against oneself. Nature must be punished for continuing to rebel, despite all the best efforts of the Nazi mind. And the more material reality challenges the Nazi's delusion of his power over Nature, or even that the Jew is not to blame for the failure of that power, the more cruelly will the Nazi punish the Jew. Because continually and without pause Nature continues to challenge his idea of who he is, the Nazi organizes the concentration camp in order to break the heart and spirit of the Jew. It is the human heart the Fascist would destroy, for this same heart resonates with every other living being, with the atmosphere itself, with the rise of the sun, the seasons: this heart partakes of every birth.

The Nazi expresses a special fury towards creation itself. On the one hand celebrating and encouraging what he calls 'Aryan Birth', the Nazi expresses his covert fear and hatred of procreation itself by performing what he calls scientific experiments on Jewish men and women aimed at the genital and reproductive organs. In this way he can punish both sexual feeling and the cycle of life and death, the fact of human mortality which we associate with birth. He orders the sterilization of Jewish men and women. And this is only the first step in a programme he plans of genetic management designed to create what he calls 'racial purity'. He believes that his enemy is trying through miscegenation to enter the very bloodstream of the German nation, for of course the other is in the bloodstream, is in fact the very heart of the self. And in violation of the strongest feelings of compassion that are in the human heart, striking out against human empathy itself, the Nazi puts pregnant women and small children to death, at the beginning of what he calls the 'Final Solution'.

We can recognize in Hitler's madness a self-portrait of this civilization which has shaped our minds. Today modern science makes the same attempt to control procreation through genetic engineering. And (in *Reclaim the Earth* in an article by Rosalie Bertrell) one reads that radiation causes genetic mutation and sterility. Thus civilization continues to rage at procreation. And today we also share with the Nazi mind a plan for a final solution to the problem of Nature. And this solution is to destroy Nature and replace Nature with a record of her destruction. One sees this pattern again and again in history. Despite the fact that the Third Reich attempted to hide the existence of concentration camps from international scrutiny, the atrocities committed in them were carefully documented by the SS. Hitler used to watch films in his private rooms of men and women being murdered and tortured. The same hidden motive, to destroy the natural and replace Nature with culture, can be seen in the pornographic snuff film, in which it is advertised that a woman is actually murdered. In one classic pornographic film called *Peeping Tom*, the hero is a cameraman whose camera is armed with a spear, and when he photographs a woman, his camera murders her and he makes a record of her death agony. When Jack the Ripper learned that a police photographer was working on his case, he arranged the bodies of his victims into compositions to be photographed. Thorough records of the cruelties committed aboard the slave ships and in slavery were kept by the slave-traders and slave-owners themselves, and the best documentation of the massacre of American Indians has been kept by the United States Army.

Today United States military strategists have developed a new plan for winning a nuclear war. They argue that the winner of a nuclear war will be the side which has kept the best record of destruction, the side which knows the most about what has taken place. Hence intelligence-gathering devices are being prepared for launching into space, where these machines will not be destroyed. These men have actually confused their own physical survival with the survival of information.

It is in the nature of the deluded mind to choose to preserve its delusion over its own life. When the German armies were faltering on the Russian Front, Hitler diverted troop and supply trains from that crucial battle in order to carry women, men and children to Auschwitz to their deaths. He imagined his war against the Jew to be more important. And this was the real war in which his mind was engaged – a war, in fact, with himself.

For Hitler's personal hatred for the Jew was a covert hatred of a part of self. In *Mein Kampf*, Hitler described the moment when he became an anti-semite. He said that when he was walking the streets of Vienna he saw an old Jewish man in a kaftan. He asked himself, 'Was the man Jewish?' and then decided that the question properly should be, 'Was this man German?' It was necessary for Hitler to define this man as 'not German', and thus unlike himself. How else could he project qualities in himself which he wished to deny onto this man, unless he defined him as unlike himself, as not German. This idea that Jews were not German became part of the Nazi propaganda campaign and even the educational system. In his orations, Hitler speaks frequently of the man in the kaftan, making this stranger a symbol of his hatred for the Jews. Yet what Hitler's biographers reveal is that as a young art student, poor and unable to buy new clothing, he brought his clothing second-hand from a Jewish man, and the article of clothing he wore most often, one which his friends began to identify him with, was a kaftan. If we look upon Hitler's personal illness as both an effect of and an expression of a national illness, it will not be surprising to discover that the kaftan was actually medieval German dress which the Jews adopted before an earlier period of exile, and then kept during exile and after their return to Germany. A whole nation failed to recognize an image of itself.

But this is also true of our civilization as a whole. We do not know ourselves. We try to deny what we know. We try to break the heart and the spirit of Nature, which is our own heart and our own spirit. We are possessed by an illness which is created by our minds, an illness which resembles sado-masochism, schizophrenia, paranoia – all the forms of the troubled soul. We are divided from ourselves. We punish ourselves. We are terrified of what we know and who we are. And finally, we belong to a civilization which is bent upon suicide, which is secretly committed to destroying Nature and destroying the self that is Nature.

The sources of fossil fuel began to dwindle. We learn that soil becoming dependent on this source for its enrichment loses the ability to replenish itself. We learn that nitrogen fertilizer harms the environment, leads to the pollution of water and the death of species. Yet we continue in this method of farming, despite massive documentation that it is a suicidal course. For we persist in the belief that we are not, like the soil itself, living; we deny that the spirit we express through culture is embedded in matter; we believe that we can survive only by manipulating Nature. And we use our understanding only for this purpose. We do not understand the meaning of our knowledge, but we use it simply as power. We do not even know ourselves; we both fear and hate ourselves. And we form a relationship to the earth that is like the witchburner torturing a witch, or Francis Bacon interrogating Nature, or the Nazi doctor performing an experiment on the prisoner of a concentration camp. If documents exist which tell us that we are destroying Nature, this does not change our behaviour, for this is our secret intent.

But we each have another secret too, a secret knowledge of wholeness. The schemata of memory excludes our memory of childhood. We do not think we still know what it was to be a child, untaught by culture to be divided from ourselves. Yet within each of us, in our bodies, that memory still exists – even though we have attempted to obliterate the landscape and replace it with the geometric city. The earth itself still reminds us of a woman's body, of our own bodies, of what it

199

is to exist in communion with the mother's body. Our own breath reminds us of that knowledge, of a time when we were curious, when we let Nature speak to us and in us.

There exists a culture which is not alienated from Nature but which expresses Nature. The mind is a physical place. The mind is made up of tissue and blood, of cells and atoms, and possesses all the knowledge of the cell, all the balance of the atom. Human language is shaped to the human mouth, made by and for the tongue, made up of sounds which can be heard by the ear. And there is to the earth and the structure of matter a kind of resonance. We were meant to hear one another, to feel. Our sexual feelings, our capacity for joy and pleasure, our love of beauty move us towards a love which binds us to all existence. If there is a sound-wave anywhere on this earth, if there is the sound of weeping or of laughter, this reaches my ears, reaches your ears. We are connected not only by the fact of our dependency on this biosphere and our participation in one field of matter and energy, in which no boundary exists between my skin and the air and you, but also by what we know and what we feel. Our own knowledge, if we can once again possess it, is as vast as existence.

I am a woman born in and shaped by this civilization, with the mind of this civilization, but also with the mind and body of a woman, with human experience. Suffering grief in my own life, I have felt all the impulses that are part of my culture in my own soul. In my resistance to pain and change, I have felt the will towards self-annihilation. And still the singing in my body daily returns me to a love of this earth. I know that by a slow practice if I am to survive, I must learn to listen to this song.

X

A New Approach to Biology

Rupert Sheldrake

Today, 22 October 1983, with several million people throughout Europe taking part in demonstrations in support of United Nations Disarmament Week and protesting against plans to deploy yet more nuclear weapons in Europe, it is impossible not to be aware of the increasing danger with which we are faced. It seems to me that unless we change the way we think and feel, the chances of our own survival and the survival of countless other living organisms on this planet are remote. I hope that today we can reflect a little more about this question of our attitudes and the influence they have.

Before going on to this I would like to consider briefly some of the problems of biology, and in particular a new way of thinking about these problems provided by the hypothesis of formative causation. This has many wide-ranging implications and I think some of them are relevant to the question of our attitude to nuclear armaments.

The hypothesis starts with some of the central problems of biology. It is not something that has been conjured out of thin air, but which has grown out of a whole tradition of biological thought and research which has been going on for well over a century. One of the central problems of biology is to understand how animals and plants grow and develop. Some of the most simple and obvious things about living organisms that we see every day are the least understood: plants grow from seeds, embryos develop, mothers give birth, and so on. In these processes, living forms appear. They only appear from something that is already living, a fertilized egg for example, but what they grow from is usually far simpler than what they become. As organisms develop, a tremendous complexity of structure and form appears, and then in the case of animals a great richness of behaviour unfolds. Think of the instincts of insects like bees or ants, or how young spiders can spin webs without ever learning it from their parents, or the way in which birds migrate instinctively to distant parts of this planet. All these very obvious things about plants and animals, as well as a great deal about ourselves, are not at all understood in terms of existing science.

The mechanistic theory of life, which forms the basis of conventional biology, says that living organisms are nothing but complicated machines, and that the whole is nothing but the sum of the parts. Therefore the aim of mechanistic biology is to reduce the organisms to the parts and their interactions, and finally to reduce the whole of biology to physics. This programme has been quite successful in some areas, and the reason why it is so influential is because of its success. Some parts of the body are indeed like machines – the heart is like a pump, the lungs are like bellows, the eyes a bit like a camera, the brain in some ways resembles a telephone exchange with wires coming in and going out, the arms work like levers, and much of the chemistry of living organisms follows standard kinds of chemical pathways. We have amino acids, ketones, aldehydes, sugars and many other identifiable chemicals in our bodies. We now know the chemical constitution of the genetic material, DNA; we know a lot about the way in which proteins are made and about their structure. Moreover, there have been great successes in medicine and of course modern mechanistic medicine is based on mechanistic biology.

But there are other areas where this approach has been unsuccessful. Many people assume that the basic problems of life are already solved. But they are not. For example, as I have just mentioned, there is the mystery of the coming-into-being of form. We can see the problem a little more clearly if we just think of our own bodies. Consider the arms and legs. The chemicals inside them are identical; the muscles, the bones, the proteins are chemically the same in both, and so is the DNA – indeed the genetic material is identical in all the cells in our bodies. Yet in spite of their chemical identity the arms and the legs have a different shape. Their shape is not explained by the chemicals they contain, just as the buildings we see out of the window are not entirely explained in terms of the stone they are made out of. The form depends both on the materials *and* on the way the materials are organized. The organization of the material, the formal structure, is not reducible to the things it is made out of. With the same stones and the same wood and the same tiles one could make buildings of different form, just as with the same chemicals the arms and the legs have different shapes.

What is it that gives organisms their form? When we walk in the countryside we see dozens of different kinds of plant. All of them are living in the same earth, getting the same sunlight, with the same carbon dioxide in the air and using the same water from the soil. Yet their forms are different, and each species has its own kind of form and organization. What is this due to?

Because attempts to explain form and structural organization in terms of chemistry have been so unsuccessful, mechanistic biology has for years retreated into a rather obscurantist position. Living shapes and patterns are said to come about through complex patterns of chemical and physical interaction which are not yet fully understood. It is simply assumed that all these things will be understood in terms of ordinary physics and chemistry at some unspecified time in the future. So the resigning paradigm is not one of rigorous mechanistic explanation, but rather what Sir Karl Popper has described as 'of promissory materialism'. It involves issuing promissory notes against future explanations which don't yet exist. In my opinion they never will, because I don't think these problems can be solved by mechanistic methods. This is where I differ from many of my biological colleagues. They admit that these are open questions, that the problems are unsolved, but they think that, given more research along conventional lines, completely mechanistic answers will be found in the end.

However, there has been a long dissident tradition within biology of scientists who have felt that the phenomena of life can't be adequately explained simply in terms of physics and chemistry. One reason for thinking this is because organisms have a curious kind of wholeness, which is more than the sum of their parts. This can be shown most easily by taking parts away. For example if a leg is cut off a newt, a part has gone. But then the rest of the newt regenerates the leg and you get a whole back again. Or if the lens is cut out of a newt's eye, the eye grows a new lens. The lens in this case forms from the edge of the iris, whereas normally, in the embryo, it forms in a different way by a folding in of the outside skin. If you cut a flatworm into small pieces, each piece can become a new worm; and of course if you cut a plant into bits, you can grow many new plants. From one tree you can produce thousands of trees – each part that you took off as a cutting can become a new tree. The parts can become wholes.

We are often deluded by people telling us that with computers and cybernetics, living processes such as these can be modelled. But we have to think not of some abstract computer model, but of the actual thing. The actual thing that people are talking about in the computer analogy is the computer and its activities. And you can see that if you cut a computer into small pieces you don't get lots of small wholes which will regenerate. You simply get a broken computer.

A concept which has been developed over the last 60 years forms the starting point for my hypothesis. This is the idea of morphogenetic fields. *Morphe* means form and *genesis* means coming into being; so morphogenesis is the coming-into-being of form. These fields were assumed to be involved in the coming-into-being of form in animals and plants. The idea was that as an organism developed it would be shaped or moulded by these morphogenetic fields, which are invisible structures around it. These fields were thought of by analogy with the known fields of physics, which are all invisible structures. None of us has ever seen, touched, tasted, smelt or heard one. We forget, because they are part of ordinary science, that they are really very extraordinary. The idea of morphogenetic fields takes the idea of invisible structures one step further in proposing a new kind of field that works in living organisms. The idea has the great advantage of helping to explain where the form and structure of the organism comes from – from the field. It also helps to account for the holistic properties of organisms, because fields have a holistic quality. Think of a magnet surrounded by a magnetic field. You can't cut a slice out of that field: the field is a whole. If you cut a magnet into two, you get two whole magnets, small ones. You don't get a north pole and a south pole isolated from each other. And each fragment of the magnet is a magnet itself with a full magnetic field around it. So this property of fields could also help to account for regeneration and the wholeness of organisms.

A very attractive idea. But it is open to the obvious objection that if we explain all these things in terms of fields, then how do we explain the fields themselves? Where do they themselves get their structure from? One way of answering this is to say that they have always had it, that they are in effect Platonic archetypes, or eternally given forms. Some biologists have indeed adopted this point of view. I myself prefer to think more in terms of causal explanations which can be tested. The basis of the hypothesis I am putting forward is that morphogenetic fields derive their structure from the actual structure or forms of previous members of a species. A cat morphogenetic field, for example, which shapes the embryonic kitten as it grows, is derived from the actual forms of previous cats. This involves a kind of causal influence of like upon like through space and time, direct connections by a process which I call morphic resonance. The morphogenetic fields therefore act as a kind of collective memory of the species in which the forms, patterns and structures of the species are carried. All organisms within the species are shaped by these fields, and in turn through their actions and activities contribute to them.

The hypothesis also applies to forms of non-living things such as crystals; I am suggesting that crystals are also moulded and shaped by morphogenetic fields. At the other end of the scale, not only the organization of form and structure but also the behaviour and instincts of animals depend on three fields.

This hypothesis leads to a range of startling predictions. This is what makes it scientific, because a scientific hypothesis must be able to be tested empirically. And this hypothesis can be tested in many different ways, and is indeed being tested at present.

In the realm of crystals, the hypothesis predicts that if you make a new chemical compound that has never existed before, there will not already be a morphogenetic field for its crystals, because those crystals have never yet formed. In order to crystallize it, you may just have to wait for a morphogenetic field to come along, and sooner or later the compound crystallizes. After this, the next time the compound is crystallized anywhere in the world, it should happen somewhat more easily because of an influence from the first crystals; the third time easier still, and so on. In this way, there will be a cumulative influence from previous crystals, and this means, according to the hypothesis, that it should get easier to crystallize the same compound all over the world as time goes on.

Is this true? In fact, it is well known to chemists that new compounds are generally very difficult to crystallize, and as time goes on they get easier and easier to crystallize all over the world. One possible reason is that people get to know how to do it, but the most popular explanation is that this happens because fragments of previous crystals which act as seeds for further crystallization are carried around the world on the clothing or the beards of migrant chemists! These stories don't appear in chemistry text books, but they are very much part of the folklore of chemistry. When one speaks to chemists one is often told these kinds of anecdote. In cases where there haven't been any migrant chemists, it is simply assumed that microscopic fragments of crystals go into the air, were wafted around the world in the atmosphere and have then settled in laboratories in remote parts of the globe.

Well, this hypothesis, the conventional one, has never been tested. It could be; and so I simply propose experiments whereby new compounds be crystallized under standard conditions in dust-free rooms from which bearded chemists are excluded. Then one would be able to see whether in the absence of these known kinds of influence crystallization still occurs more readily. If it does, it will provide good evidence for the hypothesis I am proposing. These experiments can be done quite cheaply, quite simply, in ordinary chemistry laboratories.

The hypothesis makes many predictions in relation to the form of animals and plants, but the easiest to understand concern behaviour. Here I come to the well-known example of rats. The hypothesis predicts that if animals, such as rats, learn a new trick in one place, rats of the same breed should be able to learn the same trick more quickly everywhere else in the world, even in the absence of any known kind of connection or communication. The more rats that learn it in one place, say Bristol, the easier it should become everywhere else. You may think, if this is true, why haven't people noticed it? The answer is that they have. The copious literature on rat psychology that has been built up over the last few decades contains several examples. I describe in my book, *A New Science of Life*, a particularly interesting series of experiments carried out in America, Scotland and Australia. In these experiments, rats were put in a water maze from which they had to escape in a particular way. At first, the rats learned only slowly to do this, but as time went on the rate of learning increased all over the world. This happened not only in rats descended from parents which had learned the task, but in all the rats of that breed. By the end of this series of tests, rats were learning on average about ten times faster than their predecessors.

One of the advantages of experiments of this kind, involving whole organisms, is that they are actually quite cheap to do. Some of the experiments I am proposing with fruit flies, for example, could be done on a budget of about £50, with simple equipment that could be found in most school laboratories. I just add this as an aside, because in the context of a Schumacher Lecture I think the fact that testing this hypothesis could be done so cheaply is an interesting point. It seems to be a general rule that in biology if you study whole organisms, it is usually rather inexpensive. It is only when you start breaking them down into small bits that it becomes more complicated and costly. To study the behaviour of rats, for example, all you need are rats and cages, and maybe some simple gadgets for them to learn to operate. You also need a notebook and a pencil, and of course food for the rats and all that sort of thing, but nothing very expensive. If you want to study the cells of a rat, then you need to have a microscope and equipment costing maybe a few thousand pounds. But if you want to study the molecules within them, then you need much more the sophisticated apparatus of biochemistry and molecular biology, which costs a great deal. To study the atoms, you need all the panoply of a modern physics laboratory; and to study bits of the atoms, the sub-atomic particles, you need particle accelerators miles long that cost hundreds of millions of pounds. So as a general rule the smaller and the more fragmented the things you study, the more expensive and specialized the process becomes.

To study animals and plants as wholes is usually not only quite cheap, but it is also within the capacity of people who need not be qualified specialists. It turns out that many of the tests that can be done to test the hypothesis of formative causation could in fact be done quite cheaply and simply, and this means that the process of testing the theory need not be confined to professional scientists. In fact, a prize of $10,000 is being offered by the Tarrytown Group of New York for the best test of the theory, and this competition is open to everyone.

One way of thinking about the influence of morphogenetic fields is by analogy with a television set. This is important in that it helps us to understand that *both* physical and chemical components *and* morphogenetic fields are involved in living organisms. Consider the form of the organism to be like the pictures on the screen of the set. To understand these pictures you have to take into account the set itself, with all the right wires and components connected up in the right way, and you also need to consider the energy which comes from the plug or from batteries. But in addition there are the invisible fields to which the set is tuned, through which the transmissions come. You have a tuning system, and you have the fields to which it is tuned. I think in living organisms the DNA, proteins, and other chemicals are rather like the wires and transistors of the TV set. They are the components. The way they are organized and what happens with the organization depend on the morphogenetic fields to which they are tuned. This concept leads to a very different view of heredity from the conventional one. Not only do we inherit chemicals from our forebears, such as DNA, the genetic material, but we also inherit morphogenetic fields which mould our form and influence our patterns of behaviour. These are given directly by morphic resonance from past members of the species, not by chemical inheritance. Change the chemical inheritance and you can change the tuning system, rather like a TV set being switched to another channel.

So genetic changes can and do indeed affect heredity, but this does not mean that everything is coded inside the genes, any more than the people you see on the screen are coded inside the wires and components of the television set.

This hypothesis also leads to a reinterpretation of evolutionary theory, which is based at present on the chemical theory of inheritance. Morphic resonance would allow for an inheritance of acquired characteristics, not only in the descendants of organisms which have acquired them, but in other members of the species as well, maybe in quite different parts of the world.

One of the most intriguing implications of the idea of morphic resonance concerns memory. It is conventionally assumed that memories are stored inside the brain, and of course most of us have been brought up with that assumption. The way in which they are stored is very much a matter of dispute. Some people think memories are stored in chemicals, such as RNA; others think they are stored by means of complicated electrical echoes or reverberations within the brain; and a perennial favourite is the idea of modifications of the nerve endings. However, attempts to locate memory traces within the brain have failed and it is now usually assumed that their position cannot be pinned down; they seem to be both everywhere and nowhere in particular. These puzzling findings have led to the holographic theory of memory storage, which tries to explain why you can't find localized memory traces.

Loss of memory can of course result from brain damage, but this doesn't prove that memories are stored inside the parts of the brain that are damaged. Think of the television again. If you damaged a television tuning circuit, you might lose the ability to tune in to one channel – say, ITV. But that doesn't prove that all the ITV programmes are stored inside the components that are damaged; it merely proves that they are necessary for the tuning process. There is in fact no convincing evidence that memories are stored inside the brain; the main reason why most people do not question this assumption is that there does not seem to be any other way memory could work.

However, once one begins to take seriously the idea of morphic resonance, then the possibility arises that memories may not be stored inside the brain at all. Morphic resonance works on the basis of similarity. The specificity of tuning to past similar organisms depends on how similar they are. If you think which organism in the past, perhaps an hour or a year ago, was most similar to yourself, the answer has to be *yourself*. We are more similar to ourselves in the past than we are to any other organism, and I believe this means that we are tuned in specifically to our own pasts, and why our own pasts have a predominant influence upon us.

But if we tune in directly to our own past stories, and if our memories are not stored inside our brains, then why don't we tune in to other people's pasts as well? I think the answer is that we do. According to this theory, it would be only natural to assume that we tune in to the memories of innumerable past members of our species, and that there is a kind of pooled or collective memory that we draw upon. This would consist of the basic structures of experience and thought. I would, in a word, contain archetypal patterns. And here we arrive at a concept very similar to that of Jung's idea of the archetypes in the collective unconscious. Jung thought of the collective unconscious as a memory of the species, based on an interconnection of all human consciousness. This idea makes no sense at

212

all in terms of mechanistic biology, but in terms of the ideas I am putting forward, it fits quite naturally.

It is also possible that we might tune in to the recent memories of a particular person, somewhere else, maybe only a second ago. In this case we would have something like thought-transference or telepathy. Again, such phenomena have no place in the mechanistic view of the world, but some of them would fit in with the kind of view I am putting forward. This would open up the possibility of building a bridge between science and some of the phenomena of parapsychology.

If there is a collective human consciousness and if these principles apply to people in the way that I believe they apply to animals and plants, then it should mean that we ourselves are continually exposed to these kinds of influence from other people. For example, these principles should be operative in the learning of skills. I think it should be easier to learn to ride a bicycle today than it was 100 years ago, and indeed it does seem to be the case that most children learn more easily than they used to. Of course, bicycle designs have improved, teaching methods and motivation have changed, and it is very difficult to know what balance of factors is responsible. The same would apply to new sports like windsurfing, where people seem to be learning more quickly than they did even ten years ago, and similarly to learning to play video games and to children learning to programme computers. However, to obtain more rigorous evidence, it is necessary to design tests where one can actually exclude other factors, and see whether morphic resonance, or something like it, really does apply to human behaviour.

I have recently conducted an experiment, with the help of Thames Television, which was designed to shed light on just this question. The experiment involved pictures containing hidden images. Once you have seen the hidden image in such a picture, it is very clear. There is a kind of *gestalt* effect; you suddenly get it, and once you've got it you can't not see it. This is a very rapid kind of learning. In this experiment we had two pictures, both of them new ones, both containing hidden images. These were sent to various places in the world where they were shown to groups of people under standard conditions. The number of people who could spot the hidden image within one minute in each of these pictures was recorded. One of the pictures was then shown on ITV on the afternoon of 31 August to about two million viewers who were asked to look at it, and then the answer was given. Did this change that took place in the minds of over a million people when they saw what the picture was meant to be affect other people? Apparently it did.

People in different parts of the world were tested with both pictures after the TV broadcast, not knowing which had been shown on television; nor did the people testing them know. There was no significant change in the percentage of those seeing the control picture, which had *not* been shown on television; but there was a definite and statistically significant increase in those who saw the picture that *had* been seen on television. (For a fuller account of this experiment, see the *New Scientist*, 27 October 1983). I wouldn't claim too much for this preliminary test, except to say that it does suggest that it would be worth doing again. Plans are now afoot to repeat an experiment of this type in Britain, Sweden and in other countries during the course of the coming year.

This illustrates that the question of the interconnectedness of human consciousness is susceptible to scientific investigation. I think that if such experiments

214

can be repeated, and give clear, positive results, it could be proved that some kind of influence like this is actually taking place. It may take several years before this can be established, but it is very possible that it could be.

One of the implications of this possibility is the idea that our thoughts and our attitudes can have an influence upon other people at a distance, without our knowing it. This kind of idea has been brought up in connection with the nuclear debate in a book called *The Hundredth Monkey* by Ken Keyes. This is based on a story about monkeys on an island off the coast of Japan which learned to wash sweet potatoes, supplied to them by scientists. At first one monkey started doing it, then it spread through the colony. Then, the story goes, once the number doing it had reached a particular threshold, say a hundred, monkeys on other islands in other places started doing the same kind of thing. The Hundredth Monkey story is a powerful modern myth. As evidence for an unseen interconnectedness, it is not as impressive as it seems at first, because the spread of this behaviour to other islands would have depended on the scientists going there first and throwing sweet potatoes to the monkeys. Nevertheless, it is a story which has had a tremendous influence in the last few years. Many of you are familiar with it, I am sure, and it illustrates graphically the kind of principle I am talking about.

I think the fact that this story has become so popular shows that many people are receptive to this kind of idea. This is not really surprising, because many traditional systems of thought have emphasized the interconnectedness of consciousness. In St Thomas Aquinas, the leading theologian of the Middle Ages, the idea that all humanity is, in a sense, one person was a central concept; and indeed, in Christian theology in general, individual human consciousness is not regarded as separate. This is also a central feature of the teachings of many present-day teachers, for example Krishnamurti, who often says 'I am humanity', meaning his consciousness is not separate from the rest of human kind. Susan Griffin referred to a similar idea this morning when she spoke of the effect we have on others by a kind of resonance. And it is not just within spiritual traditions that views of this kind have been held. For example, Jean-Paul Sartre wrote in *Existentialism and Humanism* as follows: 'When we say that man is responsible for himself, we do not mean that he is responsible only for his own individuality, but that he is responsible for all men . . . Our responsibility is thus much greater than we had supposed, for it concerns mankind as a whole.'

I think this is very relevant to us at the present time, because all of us are responsible for the nuclear arms race. We may not like it. We may not actively endorse it, but all of us are responsible. We live in a society where these weapons are being made and prepared for use. We are all helping to pay for them. Even if we don't pay income tax, every time we make a telephone call we are paying Value Added Tax, and all taxes in however small a way help to finance the construction of these bombs and missiles.

Some people think that the best way to maintain peace is to prepare for war. Some people sincerely believe that. Others don't. I am among those who don't believe it, but insofar as we allow the process of nuclear armament to continue, we are implicitly supporting it. This process is not just maintaining a balance of terror. We have reached a point where the destructive power of Western and Soviet nuclear weapons is totally beyond imagination. We now have over 6,000 times as much destructive power as that used in the entire Second World War. And the United States, NATO and the Soviet Union are still hurrying to increase their nuclear arsenals. This, of course, is done in the name of security, but we can hardly say that it makes us more secure. Pershing IIs take three to eight minutes to reach Russia from Germany. The minimum time in which Russian computers can be checked to see whether they are giving a false alarm is ten minutes. So the chances of nuclear war by accident are enormously increased, and will be further increased by the continuing deployment of yet more missiles over the next few years.

The whole thing can easily seem hopeless, as if we are helplessly heading towards a collective suicide. It seems obvious to me, as it does to many others, that the only real hope is a change in the way we think and feel. We now have a choice between a positive transformation of humanity, or a sudden and unintended transformation through death and destruction. We cannot postpone this choice much longer.

Fear and suspicion have brought out the worst in the Western world – a vast build-up of the power to kill, and the willingness to use it. And this feeds the fear and suspicion of the other side, who react in a similar way. Both sides bring out and encourage the evil in the other. Surely no positive change can possibly come about through more fear, suspicion and hatred. How could this happen but through faith, hope and love?

We all have a responsibility not only for what we do, or don't do; not only as citizens of states which are making and preparing to use these weapons; not only as people who have the privilege to live in democracies where we have some control over what our governments do; but we are also responsible for our innermost thoughts. If we despair, feeling that there is nothing we can do, that it is all utterly hopeless and inevitable, this attitude itself may spread and influence others. And despair and hopelessness can only help to bring about what we most fear. But if we have hope, and faith in the possibility of a new order of things, not only will our actions be more positive, but our hope and faith themselves may spread. Our responsibility may indeed be even greater than we had supposed.

Mother of All
An Introduction to Bioregionalism

Kirkpatrick Sale

To Gaea, mother of all of life and oldest of the gods,
    I sing,
You who make and feed and guide all creatures of
    the earth,
Those who move on your firm and radiant land,
    those who wing
Your skies, those who swim your seas, to all these
    you have given birth;
Mistress, from you come all our harvests, our chil-
    dren, our night and day,
Yours the power to give us life, yours to take away.
    To you, who contain everything,
    To Gaea, mother of all, I sing.
                        Homeric *Hymn to Earth*

In the beginning, as the Greeks saw it, when chaos
settled into form, there was a sphere, aloft, floating
free beneath the moist, gleaming embrace of the sky
and its swirling drifts of white cloud, a great vibrant
being of green and blue and brown and grey, binding
together in a holy, deep-breasted synchrony the temperatures of the sun, the gases of the air, the chemicals
of the sea, the minerals of the soil, and bearing the
organized, self-contained and almost purposeful aspect
of a single organism, even a living, breathing body, a

219

heart, a spirit, a soul, a goddess – in the awed words of Plato, 'A living creature, one and visible, containing within itself all living creatures.'

To this the Greeks gave a name: Gaea, the earth-mother. She was the mother of the heavens, Uranus, and of time, Cronus; she was the mother of the Titans and the Cyclops, of the Meliae, the ash-tree spirits who were the progenitors of all humankind; she was the mother of all, first of the cosmos, creator of the creators. She became the symbol of all that was sacred and the font of all wisdom, and at the fissures and rifts in her surface – at Delphi, especially, and Dodona and Piraeus – she would impart her knowledge to those oracles who knew how to hear it. And ultimately, inevitably, she became embodied in the language of the Greeks as the unit of life, of birth, of origination, combined into the word *genos* to give us, in English, *genesis, genus, genitals, genetics* and *generation*.[1]

'Earth is a goddess', wrote Xenophon in the fourth century before Christ, 'and teaches justice to those who can learn.' Justice, and comparison, and prudence, and appropriateness, and harmony, all of what were later the cardinal virtues: 'The better she is served', Xenophon taught, 'the more good things she gives in return.'

All that seems obvious enough, or at least was obvious enough to those who first inhabited the earth and created her cultures – which is why, in virtually every early society that we know of, in every preliterate society that has been discovered, the primary deity, worshipped before all others, was the earth. And even in those societies that eventually came to displace the

1. It is from Gaea, of course, that we also get our word for geography, a subject now almost as lost in the schools as the respect for the object it names, as well as *geometry* (the study of lines of the earth), *geomancy* (divination by lines of the earth), *geology, geodesy*, and the like.

earth-goddess with other gods, most typically the sky-god – a male figure, be it noted, and one adopted almost exclusively by those cultures (even the later Greeks) that simultaneously created empire, war, hierarchy, priesthood and slavery – even in those societies the earth was still considered a living being, sentient and organic, and still retained its character as a deity.

It was not until the developments of European science, from about the 16th century on, that this animistic conception of the earth finally gave way, to be replaced by one supported by the new insights of physics, chemistry, mechanics, astronomy and mathematics. The new perception held – more than that, in fact it *proved* – that the earth, the universe and all within it operated by certain clear and calculable laws and not by the whims of any living, thinking being; that, far from being divine and omnipotent, these were capable of scientific prediction and manipulation; and that objects, from the smallest stone to the Earth itself and the planets beyond, were not animate with souls and wills and purposes, but were nothing more than the combination of certain chemical and mechanical properties. The cosmos was in no sense like a purposeful, pulsatory celestial thing alive but rather, in the Newtonian image, something more like a giant clock, its many parts moving in an ordered, kinetic, mechanical way. Europe's scientific revolution – in the triumphant words of 17th-century physicist Robert Hooke – enabled humankind 'to discover all the secret workings of Nature, almost in the same manner as we do those that are the productions of [human] Art and are manag'd by Wheels, and Engines, and Springs.'

Now, as I am sure you know, the history of ideas is just like the history of technologies: those that suit the powers-that-be are embraced, those that seem to have no utility are forgotten.[2] The ideas of the new science were very quickly heeded, and their creators rewarded and pantheonized by a European establishment that at the same time was in the process of creating other complementary attitudes and systems for which scientism provided both intellectual conditioning and practical guidance. For the scientific system was developed, let us not forget, contemporaneously with – and by no means accidentally, in aid of – the consolidation of the nation state, the growth of mercantile and then corporate capitalism, and the spread of global exploitation and colonialism. Its inherent message – the celebration of the quantifiable, the mechanistic, the physiochemical, the tangible, as against the organic, the spiritual, the creative, and the intangible – had immense importance, and far beyond the laboratories, for the European society that developed out of the 16th century. And its ultimate governing principle – that humans should not merely understand but be capable of manipulating Nature, and indeed, as Descartes put it for all of European science, be 'masters and possessors of Nature' – became deeply ingrained into not merely the scientific but all scholarly and most popular thinking in the Western world from that day to this, until by now it shapes the perceptions of our senses and the patterns of our psyches.

And if today we see the Earth as a static and neutral arena which is alterable by our chemicals and controllable by our technologies; if we see ourselves as a superior species, to whom is given the right to kill off

2. I think, in this context, of Hero of Alexandria who created a steam engine of sorts in the 3rd century BC. But the Mediterranean powers of the time had no need for such a device, having an abundance of slaves, and so it was not until the 18th century, in an England where slavery was outlawed and cheap labour unreliable, that the steam engine was reinvented and perfected.

as many hundreds of others as we wish and 'have dominion over' the rest; if we believe we have the power to reorder its atoms and reassemble its genes, to contrive weapons and machines fueled by our own invented elements and capable of destroying forever most of its organic life; if we create technologies capable of plundering its resources, befouling its systems, poisoning its air perhaps irretrievably, and altering its eons-old processes to suit our wishes; and if those who are most especially devoted to the truest nature of the Earth, those we call the ecologists, can choose to dress themselves in the cloaks of scientism to talk of Nature's *entropy* or energy *production* or food *chains* or forest *management*, or even displace the image of the biotic community with that of the mechanical eco-*system* . . . if this is our condition today, it is because, far from calling into question the scientistic view of the universe in these last four centuries, we have in fact accepted it virtually in its entirety: it has become the foundation and sustenance not only of our various social systems – of education, agriculture, medicine, religion, energy, communication, transportation – but of our most basic economic and political institutions as well.

Now, to be sure, the scientific world-view is not without its values, its uses, its triumphs even, and I think we may want to call the world a better place for our knowledge of hygiene, say, or radiotelegraphy, or immunology, or electricity. But its shortcomings, its failures, its calamitous dangers have by now become obvious, and it is surely safe to say that the path of sanity, perhaps survival, is to regain the spirit of the ancient Greeks, to once again comprehend the earth as a living creature. We need to recover the sense, as Schumacher puts it in *Good Work*, 'that man is the servant of this world, or at least a trustee', a concept that has been 'organized out of our thinking,' as he puts it, 'by the modern world', and must listen again to the two great teachers, one 'the marvellous system of living Nature' and the other 'the traditional wisdom of mankind', – teachers we have 'rejected and replaced by some extraordinary structure we call objective science.' And we must re-envision humans as participants and not masters in the biotic community, only one among many species, special perhaps in having certain skills of information-gathering and communication but not for that reason superior to those with other skills – for the human being, as Mark Twain might have said, is different from other animals only in that it is able to blush. Or needs to.

In *The Interpreters*, a book by the Irish author known as AE, written at the height of the Irish Revolution, there is a passage in which a group of disparate men, all prisoners, sit around discussing what the ideal new world should look like. One of them, the poet Lavelle, argues fervently against the vision put forth by one prisoner, a philosopher, of a global, scientific, cosmopolitan culture. 'If all wisdom was acquired from without,' he says, 'it might be politic to make our culture cosmopolitan. But I believe our best wisdom does not come from without, but arises in the soul and is an emanation of the earth-spirit, a voice speaking directly to us as dwellers in the land.'

But to become 'dwellers in the land', to regain the spirit of the Greeks, to come to know the earth, fully and honestly, the crucial and perhaps only and all-encompassing task is to understand the place, the immediate, specific place, where we live: 'In the question of how we treat the land', as Schumacher says, 'our entire way of life is involved'. We must somehow live as close to it as possible, be in touch with its particular soils, its waters, its winds; we must learn its ways, its capacities, its limits; we must make its rhythms our patterns, its laws our guide, its fruits our bounty.

That, in essence, is bioregionalism.

Now I must acknowledge that 'bioregionalism' is not yet quite a household word – you're writing a book on *what*? my friends say – and when the Schumacher Board decided to use it as the theme of this forum we knew we ran the risk both of alienating the uninvolved and perplexing the sympathetic. But I believe bioregionalism to be a concept so accessible, so serviceable, so productive – and, after about five years, now so impelling as to have created a momentum of its own – that I feel quite confident in its use. For there is really nothing so mysterious about the components of the word – *bio*, from the Greek for life, *regional*, from the Latin for territory to be ruled, *ism*, from the Greek for doctrine – and nothing, after a moment's thought, so terribly strange in what they convey; and if initially it falls oddly on our ears, that may perhaps only be a measure of how far we have distanced ourselves from its wisdom – and how badly we need it now.

Let me spend a little time excavating this concept of bioregionalism a bit, baring and examining its several layers, as one might in looking at the strata of the earth.

All aspects of the bioregional society – and, one might imagine, a bioregional world – take their forms from that of Gaea herself. One of Gaea's many offspring, the first of all her daughters, was Themis, the goddess of the laws of nature and the mother of the seasons, and it is by a diligent study of her – her laws, her messages, her patterns as they have been established over these many uncounted millenia – that we can guide ourselves in constructing human settlements and systems. This is not, of course, an easy undertaking, for the lessons of Nature can sometimes seem confusing and even contradictory; and perhaps I have read them wrong: perhaps only more time and more opportunity to be closer to Nature, as close as the preliterate peoples who have twenty words for snow and distinguish thirty kinds of annual seasons, will allow us to learn them properly. But I think I have at least the outlines right, and I am bolstered by the knowledge that they seem to accord well with the findings of many others who have looked in this direction, not the least of whom was Fritz Schumacher himself.

I would offer, then, what seem to me to be the bioregional guidelines bearing upon what I regard as the four basic determinants of any organized civilization: scale, economy, politics and society.

Scale

I will, if I may – I always do – start with scale: the scale, the size, the dimensions of the bioregion as set by the characteristics of the Earth, by the *givens* of Nature. A bioregion is a part of the Earth's surface whose rough boundaries are determined by natural rather than human dictates, distinguishable from other areas by attributes of flora, fauna, water, climate soils and landforms, and the human settlements and cultures those attributes have given rise to. The borders between such areas are usually not rigid – Nature works with more flexibility and fluidity than that – but the general contours of the regions themselves are not hard to identify, and indeed will probably be felt, understood or sensed, in some way known to many of the inhabitants, and particularly those still rooted in the land, farmers and ranchers, hunters and fishers, foresters and botanists, and most especially, across the face of America, tribal Indians, those still in touch with a culture that for centuries knew the earth as sacred and its well-being as imperative.

Now one rather interesting thing about this is that when you start to look closely at how Nature is patterned – and I have spent a considerable amount of time doing this for North America in the last few months – you discover that you are dealing with something almost – appropriately enough – organic. For, just as bioregions normally merge with one another without hard-edged boundaries, so they overlap and even subsume one another in a complex arrangement of sizes depending upon the detail and specificity of natural characteristics. The whole matter is complex, and I do not wish today to go into all its intricacies, but let me just suggest the labels with which I propose to describe (and, I hope, to popularize) the various kinds of bioregional gradations.

The widest region, taking its character from the broadest measures of native vegetation and soil contours, may be called the *ecoregion* and will generally cover several hundred thousands of square miles over several states; it is possible to determine somewhere between forty and fifty such areas across North America. But within these ecoregions it is easy to distinguish other coherent territories that define themselves primarily by their surface features – a watershed or river basin, a valley, a desert, a plateau, a mountain range – and which we may call the *georegion*. And within these georegions, in turn, one can often locate still smaller areas, of perhaps several thousand square miles, discrete and identifiable with their own topographies and inhabitants, their own variations of human culture and agriculture, to which we may give the name *vitaregion*.

Using that terminology for our location today, we

227

would say that we are in an *ecoregion* that could be thought of as the Northeastern Hardwood, stretching (in conventional terms) from mid-New Hampshire and Vermont to mid-New Jersey, an area characterized by birch and beech in addition to conifers, largely podzol and blue podzolic soils, and a July-maximum-January-minimum rainfall. Within this territory are a number of obvious *georegions* – the Hudson watershed, the Berkshires, the Massachusetts Bay systems – and South Hadley is solidly within the Connecticut River georegion, a long, fertile valley running between the Green and Taconic Mountains on the west and the White Mountains on the east all the way down to the Long Island Sound. But there are obvious distinctions to be made within this georegion, too, for the valley here, as it broadens out from the Deerfield River on down to the Meshomasic foothills south of Hartford, is quite different from the stretch up north to the Ammonoosuc, or south in the pinched and hilly course to the Sound; and within this *vitaregion* clear differences from surrounding areas in both agriculture – tobacco, for example, and potatoes – and homoculture can be seen.

But I do not wish to dwell on such distinctions, to elaborate this cosmography, for I think at this stage of bioregional consciousness it is more important to stand aside a bit and appreciate the broad contours of the concepts than to plunge headlong into the briarbush of elaborate differences and definitions. Whether we speak of ecoregion or georegion or vitaregion, after all, we speak of bioregions, and it is that essential archetype that is most important to comprehend. For once that is done on any significant scale, then the matter of making distinctions and creating human institutions to match them can safely be left to the inhabitants, the dwellers in the land, who will always know them best. In the discussions to follow, therefore, we may imagine that bioregionalism will apply in its initial and formative phases to the largest territory, the ecoregion, and thereafter, in an evolving organic process, narrowing in scale as the perceptions become sharper and the tools more finely honed, to smaller and smaller territories, to the vitaregion and perhaps beyond, moving closer and closer to the specifics of the soil and those who live upon it.

Economy

The economy that comes into being within a bioregion also derives its character from the conditions, the laws, of Nature. Our ignorance is immense, but what we can be said to know with some surety after these many centuries of living on the soil has been cogently summarized by Edward Goldsmith, the editor of *The Ecologist*, as the Laws of Ecodynamics – to be distinguished, of course, from the scientistic Laws of Thermodynamics.

The first law is that conservation, preservation, sustenance, is the central goal of the natural world – hence its ingenerate, fundamental resistance to large-scale structural change; the second law is that, far from being entropic (that's an image rightly belonging to physics, errantly borrowed by scientistic ecologists), Nature is inherently stable, working in all times and places toward what ecology calls a *climax*: that is, a balanced, harmonious, integrative state of maturity which, once reached, is maintained for prolonged periods. From this it follows that a bioregional economy would seek to maintain rather than exploit the natural world, accommodate to the environment rather than resist it; it would attempt to create conditions for

229

a climax, a balance, for what some economists have recently taken to calling a 'steady state', rather than for perpetual change and continual growth in service to 'progress', a false and delusory goddess if ever there was one. It would, in practical terms, minimize resource-use, emphasize conservation and recycling, avoid pollution and waste. It would adapt its systems to the given bioregional resources – energy based on wind, for example, where Nature called for that, or wood where that was appropriate, and food based on what the region itself – particularly in its native, pre-agricultural state – could grow.

And thus it would be based, above all, on the most elemental and most elegant principles of the natural world, that of self-sufficiency. Just as Nature does not depend on trade, does not create elaborate networks of continental dependency, so the bioregion would find all its needed resources – for energy, food, shelter, clothing, craft, manufacture, luxury – within its own environment. And far from being deprived, far from being thus impoverished, it would gain in every measure of economic health. It would be more stable, free from boom-and-bust cycles and distant political crises; it would be able to plan, to allocate its resources, to develop what it wants to develop at the safest pace, in the most ecological manner. It would not be at the mercy of distant and uncontrollable national bureaucracies and transnational governments, and thus it would be more self-regarding, more cohesive, developing a sense of place, of community, of comradeship, and the pride that comes from stability, control, competence and independence.

In what was perhaps one of his most prescient perceptions, Fritz Schumacher realized that the market economy of 20th-century capitalism erred fundamentally, because it erred repeatedly, against Nature. 'It is inherent in the methodology of economics to ignore man's dependence on the natural world', he wrote. 'The market represents only the surface of society and its significance relates to the momentary situation as it exists there and then. There is no probing into the depths of things, into the natural or social facts that lie behind them.' And this is why, as he points out, conventional economics make no distinctions at all between primary goods, 'which man has to win from Nature', and secondary goods manufactured from them, or between renewable and nonrenewable resources, or the environmental and social costs of developing one against the other.

A bioregional economy, in sharpest contrast, makes – in fact is grounded in – these vital distinctions.

Politics

Political principles on a bioregional scale are also grounded in the dictates presented by Nature, in which what is forever valued are not the imperatives of giantism, centralization, hierarchy and monolithicity, but rather, in starkest contraposition, those of scale, decentralization, division and diversity.

Nothing is more striking in the examination of a natural setting than the absence of the forms of authoritarianism, domination and sovereignty that are taken as inevitable in human governance; even the queen bee is queen only because we designate her so. In a healthy ecological, niche, or 'econiche', the various sets of animals – whether themselves organized as individuals, families, bands or communal hives – get along with one another without the need of any system of authority or dominance – indeed, without structure or organization of any kind soever. No one species rules, not one even makes the attempt, and the only assertion of power has to do with territory, with a particular area to be left alone in. Each set, each species, in the system has its own methods of organization, but none attempts to impose them on any other or to set itself up as the central source of power or sovereignty. Far from there being contention and discord, the pseudo-Darwinian war of all-against-all, there is, for the most part, balance and adjustment, co-operation among communities, integration into the environment, variety, complexity and flexibility.

The lessons are of course obvious, and suggest immediately the design for a bioregion, as they do for a continent of bioregions. Each unit, of the size that the natural settings promote, may be unified and cohesive – let us imagine, for a start, a neighbourhood, a community, a small town – and yet live side-by-side with others in a settled and mutual pattern, together comprising a vitaregion; and that vitaregion may have its own unification and cohesiveness, its own method of governance, and yet live side-by-side with other regions, organized as they may see fit; and so on, outward, in self-sufficient collaboration, unit upon unit, for so long as the natural boundaries may permit and the natural affinities be kept intact.

Similar lessons may be derived from the patterns of *human* nature, and in the matter of political relations it is only fitting to factor those in as well. Throughout all human history, even in the past several hundred years, people have tended to live in separate and independent groups, a 'fragmentation of human society' that Harold Isaacs, the veteran MIT professor of international affairs, has described as something akin to 'a persuasive force in human affairs and always has been'. Even when nations and empires have arisen, he notes, they have no staying power against the innate human drive to fragmentation: 'The record shows that there could be all kinds of lags, that declines could take a long time and falls run long overdue, but that these conditions could never be indefinitely maintained. Under external or internal pressures – usually both – authority was eroded, legitimacy challenged, and in wars, collapse, and revolution, the system of power redrawn.'

I feel I must add here a note that may be painful for those whose allegiance to the precepts of fragmentation and diversification tend to crumble halfway through. Bioregional diversity means exactly that. It does not mean that every region of the north-east, or North America, or the globe, will construct itself upon the values of democracy, equality, liberty, freedom, justice, and other suchlike *desiderata*. It means rather that truly autonomous bioregions will likely go their own separate ways and end up with quite disparate political systems – some democracies, no doubt, some direct, some representative, some federative, but undoubtedly all kinds of aristocracies, oligarchies, theocracies, principalities, margravates, duchies and palatinates as well. And some with values, beliefs, standards and customs quite antithetical to those that the people in this room, for example, hold dearest.

Schumacher somewhere quotes with favor Gandhi's remark that it is worthless to go 'dreaming of systems so perfect that no one will need to be good.' But that is exactly what I think is *necessary*. There's no point, it seems to me, in dreaming of systems where we can expect everyone is *going* to be good, not merely because that would produce a fairly vapid society, I should think, but because there's every reason to suppose that it is simply not likely to take place on this planet in this galaxy. We must dream of systems, rather, which allow people to be *people*, in all their variety, to be wrong upon occasion and errant and bad and even evil, to commit the crimes which as near as we know have always been committed – brutality, subjugation, even war – and yet where all social and civil structures work to minimize such errancies and, what is even more important, hold them within strict bounds should they occur. Bioregionalism, properly conceived, is such a construct, because it provides a scale at which misconduct is likely to be mitigated because bonds of community are strong and material, and social needs for the most part fulfilled; at which the consequences of individual and regional actions are visible and unconcealable, and violence can be seen to be a transgression against the environment and its people in defiance of basic ecological common sense; and at which even error and iniquity, should they happen, will not do irreparable damage beyond the narrow regional limits, and will not send their poisons coursing through the veins of entire continents and the world itself. Bioregionalism, properly conceived, not merely tolerates but thrives upon the diversities of human behaviour, and the varieties of political and social arrangements those give rise to, even if at times they may stem from the baser rather than the more noble motives. In any case, there is no other way to have it.

Society

Once recently, when asked to name the seven wonders of the world, the renowned biologist Lewis Thomas led off with the extraordinary phenomenon of the Oncideres beetle and the mimosa tree. It seems that when she wishes to lay her eggs the female Oncideres beetle picks out a mimosa tree, crawls out on one of its limbs and cuts a long lengthwise slit into which she drops her sacs. Then, because in the larva stage the offspring cannot survive in live wood, she backs down the branch a foot or so and cuts a neat circular slit through the bark all around the limb, which has the effect of killing the branch within a very short time, whereupon it falls to the ground in the next strong wind and becomes the home for the next generation of Oncideres beetles. But, interestingly, this process also has the effect of *pruning* the mimosa tree, a rather valuable ancillary result because, left alone, a mimosa has a lifespan of twenty-five to thirty years, but pruned in just this simple way it can flourish for a century or more.

Now Dr Thomas seems to regard this relationship as sufficiently extraordinary to be regarded as a wonder of the world, particularly worthy, he writes, because such things 'keep reminding us of how little we know about nature.' Well, perhaps confession on the side of ignorance is wise in these matters, and yet I do think it is permissible to point out that, first, far from being unusual, this sort of biological interaction is in fact commonplace throughout every phase of Nature, and, moreover, it is found with such regularity that it should indicate at least one lesson we know very well. The relationship is called, of course, symbiosis, and its persistence and pervasiveness in the natural world should be allowed to suggest to us, if we will but let it, a fundamental principle. From the very mitochondria that float about in our cells, infinitessimal creatures with their own DNA and RNA who live on us as we live on them, right on to the giant clam which lives off the photosynthesis created by the plant cells it engulfs and actually incorporates into its body, where the cells live happily in a protected environment that even includes small lenses in the clam's tissues particularly adapted to increase their needed sunlight – from the smallest to the largest, the recurrence of the phenomenon of symbiosis provides a model, if it does not strongly suggest the need, for reordering of human society along similar lines, with families and neighbourhoods and communities and cities operating within a bioregion on the basis of collaboration, exchange, cooperation and mutuality, rather than contention, competition and selfishness.

The prime example of such an interaction on the bioregional scale would be the social symbiosis between the city and the countryside, the urban and the rural, a correlation which has been celebrated by philosophers from Aristotle on, whose interweavings have been brilliantly analyzed by the woman with whom I share the platform this morning, and whose demise has been tellingly bemoaned by all the giants of our century, from Mumford to Borsodi to Bookchin. Listen to Fritz Schumacher:

> Human life, to be fully human, needs the city: but it also needs food and other raw materials gained from the country. Everybody needs ready access to both countryside and city. It follows that the aim must be a *pattern* of urbanization so that every rural area has a nearby city, near enough so that people can visit it and be back the same day. No other pattern makes human sense.
>
> Actual developments during the last hundred years or so, however, have been in the exactly opposite direction: the rural areas have been increasingly deprived of access to worthwhile cities. There has been a monstrous and highly pathological polarization of the pattern of settlements.

'Pathological polarization'. The mixedness of the metaphor aside, that is obviously the exact opposite of symbiosis; that is equally obviously, as Schumacher saw, the condition of our time. Could we imagine a sadder comment?

236

In a bioregional society, the division between urban and rural, industrial and agricultural, population and resources, would be replaced by an equilibrium, a symbiosis. On the one hand, the city would be necessary as a producer of certain kinds of goods, as a centre of artistic culture, as a source of the assembled civic virtues, though the city need not be of immense size – indeed, no larger than 50,000 or 100,000 people – and, in fact, ideally would replicate rather than grow, so that instead of a single metropolis there would be a multiplicity of cities of modest sizes scattered throughout the bioregion. And, on the other hand, the country would of course be necessary as the prime source of food and water and the materials of shelter and clothing and artisanship and trade, and especially as the embodiment of the bioregional spirit, of Gaea, whose presence should be felt daily by the inhabitants of every settlement, of whatever size. Nor should this equilibrium suggest some sort of polarization of its own, for in a bioregional society living with, on, for and around the earth as a necessitarian matter, of course the countryside would become *part of* the city, not merely in the sense of parks and woodlands and greenswards and open waterways – as fundamental as they are – and not merely in the sense of backyard and rooftop gardens and floral displays and tree-lined streets and plaza fountains – as desirable as they are – but through the integration into every urban process of a total understanding of ecological principles, until the smallest child knows that water does not come from a pipe in the basement, and that you can't throw anything away because there is no 'away'.

Now it would be possible to continue this description of the bioregional civilization as derived from the laws

237

of Nature – as it relates to energy, for example, and agriculture, and health, and defence, and much else besides – and of course such a task is ultimately necessary for the bioregional citizenry to undertake, with study, in depth, over time. But in those four primary determinants – scale, economy, politics and society – I hope I have suggested to you the outlines of such a project and something of what it might evolve to – some of the bones, a little of the meat – so that you can appreciate its validity at least as a *philosophical* approach. Now I would like to spend a few minutes suggesting to you the ways in which the bioregional concept also establishes its validity as a *political* approach.

To my perception, honed through these many years of mid-century turmoil, bioregionalism satisfies the principal conditions of an effective political project most particularly in these respects: it is rooted in the historical realities of the past, it accords with the visible patterns of the present, and it provides desirable and workable visions of the future. I would like, all too briefly, to touch upon each of those.

Historical Realities

There is nothing more fundamentally supportive of the validity of bioregionalism than its being the modern version of a very old perception of the world held not merely by the Greeks but, as I indicated before, by virtually every preliterate society of which we have knowledge. It must mean something that the early human societies which occupied this planet for our first 50,000 years or so regarded the sacredness of the earth as a truth so profound that it could be accurately described as almost innate; it must have significance that in most subsequent societies until quite recently, the earth and its behaviour formed the basis of all folk knowledge, not merely in matters of agriculture and nutrition but in medicine, religion, art and even government. And as Schumacher says – it is indeed the ultimate sentence of *Small Is Beautiful* – 'The guidance we need for our work cannot be found in science or technology, the value of which utterly depends on the ends they serve; but it can still be found in the traditional wisdom of mankind.'

But the historical validity of this concept – the provenance, I might say, as the art dealers do in describing the history of an artwork, to establish its authenticity – can be certified in an even more concrete way, even closer to this time and place. Regionalism, whether conceived of as sectionalism, localism, separatism, agrarianism, states rights or nullificationism, has a fine and venerable tradition in this country and is, by any reckoning, as American as – depending on your region – apple, peach, Boston cream, chess, Jefferson Davis, sweet cactus, German cherry or Key lime pie.

– Frederick Jackson Turner, the great Wisconsin historian, knew it, and it formed the basis of a lifetime of studies culminating in his *The Significance of Sections in American History*, where he showed that only by a consideration of American sectional, or regional, differences could one understand the patterns of settlement, migration, architecture, literature and economic and political life: 'We in America are in reality', he concluded, 'a federation of sections rather than states.'

– Lewis Mumford knew it when he put together the Regional Plan Association in 1923, an ambitious – and, for a decade, successful – attempt to create regional plans along geographical lines that would, in his words, mean the 'reinvigoration and rehabilitation of whole regions so that the products of culture and civilization, instead of being confined to a prosperous minority in the congested centers, shall be available to everyone at every point' and so that we may 'eliminate our enormous economic wastes, give a new life to stable agriculture, and' – though I blush to say it – 'set down fresh communities planned on a human scale.'

– Howard Odum knew it when he started a highly honoured and remarkably multidisciplinary school of regionalism at the University of North Carolina in the 1930s, and over two decades produced a series of scholarly books highlighted by the massive 1938 study, *American Regionalism*, all to the point of showing, as he put it, that 'regionalism . . . represents the philosophy and technique of self-help, self-development, and initiative in which each real unit is not only aided in, but is committed to the full development of its own resources and capacities.'

– And even the United States government, *mirabile dictu*, knew it, when in 1934 it authorized a National Resource Committee to study the regions of America and discovered 'regional differentiation may turn out to be the true expression of American Life and culture [reflecting] American ideals, needs, and viewpoints far more adequately than does State consciousness and loyalty.' It was out of its exhaustive studies, more than fifteen reports in all, that the Tennesee Valley Authority was born: America's greatest – though in some respects most distorted – experiment with regionalism.

Much there is today that goes against the grain of .regionalism, of course; much forcing the nation away from its natural contours towards the artificial unanimity of a monolithic plasticized government. And yet – and yet . . . even in an age such as this, the historical realities of regionalism, as perceived by those several generations of scholars and planners, cannot be erased. And that is why, today – just to touch on a small part of this complex subject – there are more than twenty-five specialized regional governments on the TVA model operating in the US, more than a thousand metropolitan regional districts, almost 500 sub-state planning districts, and more than 100 multicounty regional associations. That is why regional planning, particularly since the 1970s, has become an established academic and governmental profession, and all but ten states now have active regional planning departments, some of which are now beginning to be responsive to bioregional imperatives. And that is why there are real and persistent rivalries among national regions for such things as defence contracts, army bases, public works projects, businesses, conventions, sports franchises and the like, a competition so strong these days that the *Wall Street Journal* this spring ran a front-page story declaring that 'another war between the states is raging.'

Contemporary Trends

Another salient measure of the validity of the bioregional enterprise is that it accords well with the most basic – and complementary – political processes in the world today: first, the pressure from a series of mounting national and global crises that threaten nothing less than the collapse of the established order, and second, the concurrent trend toward the disintegration of imperial, continental and national arrangements – what is called separatism, decentralism, or, to use a supposedly derogatory term, balkanization.

I do not need to belabour for an audience of this distinction the evidence of the crises threatening the contemporary industrial socio-capitalist system. It is sufficient, I think, merely to say that those who are predicting some sort of near-term calamity and collapse range through all the academic disciplines, from physics to philosophy, and through all the political positions, from anarchist to authoritarian. That is not enough to guarantee that such a disintegration will in fact take place, to be sure, but it is accompanied by plentiful signs of the failure of the established order to satisfy the most basic human needs of large portions of the population, of the apparently unstoppable disintegration of America's cities, and of the rising tides of poverty, disease, ignorance, anomie, suicide, violence and crime even in this most affluent of nations. And it is interesting that whatever form the collapse in fact will take, we already possess a wide variety of labels for it: Schumacher's 'the degeneration of the industrial system', Robert Nisbet's 'twilight of authority', the Club of Rome's 'oncoming age of scarcity', Arnold Toynbee's the 'end of the frontier', and, variously, 'the coming dark age', 'the twilight of capitalism', 'the biological timebomb', 'overshoot', and 'the end of the American Era'.

I remember once Fritz Schumacher, during the height of the oil crisis, looking up at the skyscrapers of New York and remarking, 'I wonder how many people will want to climb to the fortieth floor when there is not enough electricity to run the elevators?' and going on to suggest that the human limit for climbing is about four or five stories. In his typically gentle way he was encapsulating a truth: that the disintegration of the present system is coming about virtually by itself, as the era of industrial capitalism based on the exploitation of unending frontiers and nonrenewable resources – or as William Catton puts it, on its ability to steal from *elsewhere* and *elsewhen* – reaches its inevitable end; and when it does, the whole face of industrial society – the height of its buildings, the size of its cities, the extent of its markets, the reach and power of its governments, the nature of its institutions – will be forced to change, and change drastically. There is no escaping this eventual transformation, for its inevitability is programmed into the very genes of this society, part of its capitalistic DNA, if you will, and as Schumacher wrote in his final work: 'It is no longer possible to believe that any political or economic reform, or scientific advance, or technological progress could solve the life-and-death problems of industrial society.'

And the alternative society that may rise from its ashes – or, if we are terribly lucky, that will evolve before the fires of destruction actually begin and create those ashes – the one that could logically be thought of as befitting the coming age, attuned to the conditions that will prevail after the industrial society runs its course, is the bioregional.

But in a sense we do not necessarily need to wait until then, however near that 'then' is, because at least one form of the bioregional society is already taking shape, in the nascent separatist movements that have come into being in almost every corner of the globe within the last generation. They, too, represent an organic – I would argue an inevitable – response to the disintegration of the contemporary order, a growing centrifugal force as industrialism spins more wildly about. As a global phenomenon, the current rise of these movements is something quite without precedent in history; it is, according to Eric Hobsbawm, 'the characteristic nationalist movement of our time', and 'an unquestionably active, growing and powerful socio-political force.' An exhaustive elaboration would be exhausting, but it should be enough to note only the most active movements just within Europe, the continent where it might have been presumed that nations were the oldest, strongest and most cohesive: there are the Bretons, Corsicans, Occitanians and Alsatians in France, the Catalonians, Andalusians and Basques in Spain, the Welsh, Scots and Cornish in Britain, the Sicilians and Tyrolians in Italy, the Waloons and Flemish in Belgium, the Latvians, Lithuanians, Estonians, Ukrainians, Georgians and a variety of Asians in the Soviet Union, the Turks and Greeks in Cyprus, the Croatians, Bosnians, Macedonians and Montenegrins in Yugoslavia – and that, I remind you, is the bare surface.

It is truly remarkable. The undeniable trend of these last forty years has been not to larger and more consolidated arrangements, but, everywhere in the world, to smaller and more decentralized ones. In the words of Harold Isaacs, 'What we are experiencing is not the shaping of new coherences but the world breaking into its bits and pieces . . . We are refragmenting and re-tribalizing ourselves.'

And what is so interesting in this amazing process is the clear expression of the bioregional idea. For though it has long been acknowledged that the cultural aspects of these separatist movements are grounded in their special regional histories, from which they take their obvious and cherished differences of language and dress and music, the fact is that their political and social characters are every bit as rooted in the long, intimate and knowledgeable association with their particular bioregion and its history. And the truths these movements embody, the apparently unquenchable truths, are in every case the product of the lands they hold sacred.

Kirkpatrick Sale

Desirable Visions

In treading upon the insubstantial ground of the future we take certain risks, and we must face the fact that the word 'utopian' has become an epithet, a chastisement, for those who would dream of things that never were and imagine that they might still be. Yet it is a necessary part of any political construct that it offer an image of the future that can be regarded as positive and liberating and realistic and energizing. This, I submit, bioregionalism succeeds in doing.

For what the bioregional vision suggests is a way of living that not merely can take us away from the calamities of the present, the diseases of our quotidian lives, but can provide its own in-dwelling enrichments and satisfactions, a widening of human possibilities. Imagine, if you will, the joy of knowing, as we can imagine from the scholarly record, what the American Indians knew: the meaning of the changes of wind on a summer afternoon; the ameliorative properties of everyday plants; the comfort of tribal, clannish and community ties throughout life; the satisfaction of being rooted in history, in lore, in place; the excitement of a culture understandable because of its imminence in the simple realities of the surroundings. Imagine a life primarily of contemplation and leisure, where work takes up only a few hours a day – an average of less than four, according to the studies of nonliterate societies – where conversation and making love and play become the common rituals of the afternoon, and there is no scramble for the necessities of life because they are provided regularly, equally, joyfully, and without charge. Imagine a life – and here I am paraphasing an anthropologist's description of a California Indian tribe – where people feel themselves to be something other than independent, autonomous individuals . . . deeply

245

bound together with other people and with the sur-rounding nonhuman forms of life in a complex inter-connected web of being, a true community in which all creatures and all things can be felt almost as brothers and sisters . . . and where the principle of nonexploi-tation, of respect and reverence for all creatures, all living things, is as much a part of life as breathing.

But I think, however enchanting that image might be, the bioregional vision is even more important in that it actually has an air of the practical, the do-able, the achieveable: it has the smell of reality about it.

For one thing, the idea of the bioregion is accessible to people, all kinds of people, for, as Kevin Lynch notes in his *Managing the Sense of a Region*, 'our senses are local, while our experience is regional.' Lee Swen-son, an early bioregionalist, has reported that when he took his bioregional slide show across the country it didn't take long for his audiences to come up with some rough consensus about the territories they lived in that pretty well matched any ecological definition of their bioregions. If true, that suggests the process of organ-izing around this issue, especially among those outside of the usual constituencies for social change, is made much easier.

Then, too, bioregionalism joins – or at least has the potential to join – right and left (or, perhaps more precisely, it ignores right and left), and thus unites the communard with the NRA hunter, the homesteader and the conservationist, the antinuclear activist and the antipowerline farmer. The concern for place, for the preservation of Nature, the return to such traditional American values as self-reliance, local control, town-meeting democracy – these things can ally many dif-ferent kinds of political people; in fact, they have a way of blunting and diminishing other and less im-portant political differences.

Bioregionalism also has the virtue of gradualism, in that it suggests that the processes of change – of organizing, educating, energizing a following and of reshaping, refashioning, recreating a continent – are, like the overarching processes of Gaea herself, not revolutionary nor cataclysmic but, like the drift of the continents on their tectonic plates, steady, slow, continuous, regular and inevitable. One does not imagine a bioregional civilization taking place by revolutionary decree – no matter whose revolution – or even, in truth, by legislative or administrative fiat. If one had to dictate or legislate the bioregional future it would never happen, because it would be resisted and sabotaged as crazy and utopian and impractical and un-American; it is only by the long and steady tenor of evolution that people will ease themselves into such a society as the alternative futures gradually come to seem senseless and the bioregional prospect becomes the only sane choice.

And finally, the bioregional vision does not demand elaborate wrenchings of either physical or human realities. It does not posit, on the one hand, the violent interference with Nature that so many of the scientistic technofix visions of the future do – those, for example, that ask for icebergs to be floated into deserts, or the Great Plains to be given over to concentrated nuclear power plants (it does not, for that matter, have anything whatsoever to do with nuclear fission, the single most unnatural project humankind has ever devised), or rockets full of people to be fired millions of miles away into space colonies around the sun. And it does not imagine, on the other, the creation of some kind of unlikely and never-before-encountered superbeings, as do so many of the reformist and radical visions of the future – those, for example, that promise 'a new socialist man' without motives of greed or self-interest, or that plan by education or religion or therapy to evolve a populace living in aquarian harmony without human vices. On the contrary, bioregionalism insists on taking the world as it is – if anything, making it more 'as it is' – and taking people, as I indicated before, as they are.

I hope I do not suggest with all of this that the bioregional project is blind to the chances of failure – or, what is worse, half-failure – or is unmindful of the pains that might attend the accomplishment of its ends. I am not suggesting sanguinity or quiescence or detachment or passivity, just because I am suggesting hope and desirability. I mean merely to underscore that element of the project that speaks to the biblical admonition: 'Where there is no vision, the people perish.'

Lewis Thomas concludes his fascinating *Lives of a Cell* with this observation:

> Viewed from the distance of the Moon, the astonishing thing about the Earth, catching the breath, is that it is alive. The photographs show the dry, pounded surface of the Moon in the foreground, dead as an old bone. Aloft, floating free beneath the moist, gleaming membrane of bright blue sky, is the rising Earth, the only exuberant thing in this part of the cosmos. If you could look long enough, you would see the swirling of the great drifts of white cloud, covering and uncovering the half-hidden masses of land . . . It has the organized, self-contained look of a live creature, full of information, marvellously skilled at handling the Sun.

And just one year later, in 1975, the British atmospheric chemist James Lovelock described in the magazine *New Scientist* a perception of the world that had come to him and his colleagues one day:

It appeared to us that the Earth's biosphere is able to control at least the temperature of the Earth's surface and the composition of the atmosphere. Prima facie, the atmosphere looked like a contrivance put together co-operatively by the totality of living systems to carry out certain necessary control functions. This led to the formulation of the proposition that living matter, the air, the oceans, the land surface, were parts of a giant system which was able to control temperature, the composition of the air and sea, the pH of the soil and so on as to be optimal for survival of the biosphere. The system seemed to exhibit the behaviour of a single organism, even a living creature.

And out of this new perception, Lovelock and colleagues created a whole new scientific hypothesis on the nature of the biosphere. Or should I say a very old hypothesis? For when they went in search of a name for this hypothesis they sought out William Golding, the novelist who just last week was honoured with the Nobel Prize. And what did he suggest, immediately? As Lovelock writes: 'He suggested Gaea – the name given by the ancient Greeks to their earth-goddess.'

So – after all – there seems no doubt about it. The Earth, the biosphere, *is* alive, a living creature, one and visible, containing within itself all living creatures. Like any living entity it can be stressed, or injured, or diseased, as it surely is now. But it will live – of that we can be sure, one way or another, and it will resettle itself, restore itself, with humankind or without. It behoves us, as nothing in the long history of humankind, I believe, has so far behoved us, to come to this literally most vital understanding and, before it is too late, give up those demonic practices that threaten our fundamental forms of existence and ultimately our existence itself. We must make the goddess Gaea part of – no, I want to say the whole of – our lives, even though that may be, as John Todd has suggested, a change of consciousness as profound and as wrenching as that which accompanied the origination of agriculture some 10,000 years ago. But then, what other choice, really, do we have?

Notes on Contributors

JOHAN GALTUNG, born 1930, is Professor of Peace Research at the University of Oslo, founder and Director of the International Peace Research Institute, Oslo, and Editor of the *Journal of Peace Research*. He has been a professor at Columbia University, New York, and the Latin American Faculty of Social Sciences, Santiago, Chile; visiting professor in Tokyo, New Delhi, Cairo, Kampala, Zurich, and the University of Essex; consultant to UNESCO on peace research, to the OECD on education, and to the Council of Europe on European co-operation.

His publications include *Gandhi's Political Ethics* (together with Arne Naess), *Theory and Methods of Social Research, Members of Two Worlds, Co-operation in Europe*, and numerous articles on peace research problems.

SHIRLEY WILLIAMS is a founder member of the Social Democratic Party. She is a Fellow at the Policy Studies Institute, and was Secretary of State for Education in the last Labour Government.

GERALD LEACH is a Senior Fellow at the International Institute for Environment and Development, London. He is a science writer and broadcaster and was the science correspondent of the *Observer*. His study for 'A Low Energy Strategy for the UK' has been widely acclaimed. He was the Director of IIED team appointed to examine and report on long-term energy policy options for the government of the United Republic of Tanzania, working in the Office of President. The report was completed in August 1980.

COLIN WILSON was one of the 'angry young men'. He is the author of *The Outsider* and 45 other books, and was about to write a book with E. F. Schumacher just before the latter's death. Colin Wilson lives in Cornwall.

RUSSELL MEANS is a member of the Oglala Lakota tribe, and has long been a major figure in the American Indian Movement. He has organized on reservations and in cities, and he helped plan the occupation of Wounded Knee. He has been shot, injured and jailed during the state of near-war that has long existed between militant American Indians on the one side and government forces on the other. Means lives in South Dakota, USA.

WENDELL BERRY has been referred to by Ken Kesey as 'the Sergeant York charging unnatural odds across our no-man's-land of ecology.' He has taught at the University of Kentucky for many years and he and his family live and farm in Port Royal, Kentucky. He is the author or *Unsettling of America: Culture and Agriculture*, *Gift of Good Land* and *Recollected Essays*.

GARY SNYDER was born in 1930 and grew up in the rural Pacific Northwest. He graduated from Reed College in 1951 with degrees in anthropology and literature, and later (1953–56) studied Japanese and Chinese at Berkeley, returning there to teach in the English Department. He also spent a semester at Indiana University studying linguistics. After participating in the San Francisco renaissance, the beginning of the beat poetry movement, with Ginsberg, Whalen, Rexroth and McClure, Snyder went to Japan in 1956. He stayed there for a year and a half, living in a Zen temple. He is the author of *Real Work*, *Turtle Island*, *Earth Household* and many other books of poems and prose.

PETRA KELLY is one of the leading lights of West Germany's Green politics. She, together with her colleagues, has made history with the first ever ecological party to win political power and enter parliament anywhere in the world.

She was born in Bavaria and studied political science at Washington and at the European Institute in Amsterdam. She worked closely with Dr Sicco Mansholt at the EEC in Brussels. When her half-sister died of cancer at the age of 10 she became convinced of the connection between children's cancer and the nuclear and chemical industries. Ever since, she has campaigned against nuclear power and nuclear weapons in London, Berlin and Frankfurt, and has travelled extensively in many parts of the world.

She has forged strong link between ecology, non-violence, disarmament and feminism, and campaigned hard and with success to get the Green Party into German Parliament.

SUSAN GRIFFIN, of whom Adrienne Rich has said, 'She is one of a growing number of contemporary women artists who, not content simply to represent what has gone unmentioned, see their work as a force for change,' lives and works in Berkeley, California. She is a feminist poet and philosopher, mother of a daughter and author of a collection of poetry, *Like the Iris of an Eye*; a play, *Voices*;

three works of non-fiction, *Rape: The Power of Consciousness*, *Woman and Nature: The Roaring Inside Her*, and *Pornography and Silence: Culture's Revenge Against Nature*.

RUPERT SHELDRAKE created a storm when his book *A New Science of Life* was published. The editor of the respected scientific journal *Nature* called it '. . . the best candidate for burning . . .' Dr Sheldrake has developed a hypothesis that there is some mystical element in the development of living creatures, which has shocked the scientific world.

Rupert Sheldrake was a scholar of Clare College, Cambridge, where he read Natural Sciences. After spending a year as a Frank Knox Fellow at Harvard University studying philosophy and the history of science, he returned to Cambridge and took a Ph.D. in biochemistry. He was a Fellow of Clare College and Director of Studies in Biochemistry and Cell Biology from 1967 to 1973, and as the Resenheim Research Fellow of the Royal Society carried out research at Cambridge on the development of plants and on the ageing of cells.

In 1974 he joined the staff of the International Crops Research Institute for the Semi-Arid Tropics in Hyderabad in India, and worked on the physiology of tropical legume crops until 1978. He is now Consultant Plant Physiologist to the same Institute. He lived for a year and a half at a Christian ashram in South India.

KIRKPATRICK SALE is an American journalist and writer. His book, *Human Scale*, has been called the encyclopaedia of the Fourth World. He writes a regular column in *Resurgence* magazine.

Schumacher Society

The Schumacher Society was formed following the death of the economist and thinker Dr E. F. Schumacher in 1977, and exists to develop, discuss and use the momentous ideas which he introduced through his writing and speeches.

The Schumacher Society aims to help establish the importance of appropriate scale in technology and in human organization, and to co-ordinate the efforts of individuals and groups searching for ways of living which restore initiative to the individual and contribute to harmony in industrial life. It encourages the preservation of the natural environment as a basis upon which to achieve these aims and, specifically, the use of organic and non-polluting agriculture.

Through meetings, lectures and conferences the Schumacher Society disseminates understanding of and enthusiasm for the vision and ideas of E. F. Schumacher. In particular, its activities include the annual Schumacher Lectures, which are held in the autumn, usually at Bristol University. These lectures bring to audiences contributions from outstanding contemporary thinkers whose ideas have changed our attitudes towards fundamental issues in modern society. Annual Essay Awards have also been established for the best essays on 'people-centred' thinking – that is, how we can create *viable* alternatives to the impersonal and sectarian systems which have been established in our present institutions.

Resurgence magazine is closely associated with the Schumacher Society and provides a major channel for its ideas and events. *Resurgence* promotes new politics and is concerned with small nations, communities, decentralization and ethnic culture – a philosophical, ecological *and* spiritual forum. It is published in Great Britain six times a year, and is available at an annual subscription of £9.

For information about the work and events of the Schumacher Society, or for a subscription to *Resurgence* (cheques should be payable to Schumacher Society), please write to:

The Secretary,
Schumacher Society,
Ford House,
Hartland,
Bideford,
Devon.

SPONSORS: Maurice Ash; Satish Kumar (Executive Chairman); Gerard Morgan-Grenville; Hazel Henderson; Leopold Kohr; Elaine Morgan; Yehudi Menuhin; Malcolm Muggeridge; Christian Schumacher (President); Edward Goldsmith; Mrs Vreni Schumacher; John Seymour.